Thank you for supporting VillageCore!

Acknowledgments

People whose support and inspiration made this book possible

My husband Teddy, who supported me both while I played the caregiver role and with my involvement in various non-profits serving seniors, especially the Village Movement.

My son, who put up with his mom's absence and supported me daily with his unconditional love and joy. He is my ray of sunshine and hope especially during challenging times.

Brad and Karen, my chief editors for their careful review.

Brad, Amanda, Angel, Drew, Jim, Kathy, Mark, Deb, Anette, Linda and many others whose passions inspire me to help seniors and their caregivers.

Members of many organizations that who have inspired me with their energy, passion and wisdom including many non-profits in the Village Movement (VillageCore, Village to Village Network, Tierrasanta Village of San Diego, etc.), San Diego Senior Alliance, Aging 2.0, and Seenager to name a few.

All the seenagers and caregivers who inspired the stories I tell in this book.

And above all: This book is written in honor of my parents.

Table of Contents

You Are a Caregiver If

You are a caregiver
 if you are the first one they call,
 if you worry about their fall,
 if you advocate for them,
 if you listen patiently to them,
 if about them you worry,
 if they need you to be happy,
 if your presence makes them smile,
 if you are central part of their life,
You may pay someone to help them
 with daily living,
But you are the ONE they turn to
 for family caregiving.

Dear Reader,

I decided to write this book for four reasons.

First, this is my therapy for healing as a primary caregiver, now that my loving family members for whom I cared for have all passed away.

Second, I heard someone once say, "Life's tough experiences are wasted unless you tell your story to help others." These words touched my heart and are a catalyst for this book of stories.

The third reason comes from over 10 years of professional experience with non-profits serving seniors. As a society, we are just not prepared for the aging of baby boomers.

According to the PEW Research Center (Baby Boomers Retire – December 29, 2010), "Roughly 10,000 Baby Boomers will turn 65 today, and about 10,000 more will cross that threshold every day for the next 19 years."

From an article in AARP magazine (You Take Care of Mom, But Who Will Take Care of You? - August 26, 2013), "Ratio of potential family caregivers to elders needing care will plummet from today's seven caregivers for each person over age 80 to fewer than three caregivers per elderly person in 2050."

So, the third reason is to help raise awareness for the challenges we are facing as a society with our aging population.

The final reason was a coincidence that happened just a few weeks after my mom died. I met a neighbor at a local event and we decided to get together for coffee. She had been a caregiver for her mom who lived in another state. In the first two hours of our conversation, I let my guards down all the way for the first time. I laughed hysterically and cried violently. It was easy for me to relate to her experiences and vice versa. We could see the humor in our interactions with our dear moms and families. She knew my pain all too well, and I was feeling hers.

Meeting this perfect stranger, with whom a two-hour sharing of experiences conversation resulted in a huge sense of relief from grief, convinced me of the importance of writing this book.

I have chosen to write this book as a fictional biography, so I can freely share the stories inspired by my experiences and of others while protecting everyone's identities.

So, let me introduce you to Rosie and Lisa. They will be your story tellers in this book about their Journeys as caregivers.

Yasmin Zahra Shah

Dear Brave Caregiver,

We hope that this book about our journeys as caregivers is your friend in solitude.

When you feel that no one understands, may you find comfort in the fact there are many others right there in your own neighborhood on the same journey as you. When the time is right, may you have the privilege of meeting your own Lisa or Rosie to help lighten your load. In the meantime, we hope the stories we share help you in your journey as a caregiver.

Stories that will make you cry,
Stories that will bring you joy,
Stories that will make you shed some tears,
Stories that will soothe your fears.

Stories that share your despair,
Stories that help your relationships repair,
Stories that fill you with love,
Stories that help you evolve.

May these stories offer you some solutions,
as you bravely walk the lonely path of caregivers.

Your friends,

Rosie and Lisa

Chapter 1 – The Birth of This Book

Moments and Stories in the Journey of a Caregiver

My name is Rosie. I live in San Diego where the weather is always beautiful, even when there are violent thunderstorms brewing inside of you. On one such day, which happened to be a Monday in January not too long ago, Lisa was moving in as my new next-door neighbor.

After seeing her going in and out of her home for the better part of the day, I saw her leaning against her fence with exhaustion. I smiled and invited her to take a break.

"Would you like a glass of iced tea?" I asked her. I could tell that that her mind was set on getting everything put away properly in her home even though her body seemed to be saying "take a break." Luckily, the movers announced just then that they were going on a late lunch. So, she agreed to come over.

As she wearily entered my home through the garage, Lisa looked around. "Are you in the process of renovating your home?" she asked.

Fighting tears, I answered: "Yes, I guess. My mom just passed away four months ago. This was her room while she was on hospice care for the past year." Now tears were streaming down my face.

"I guess you needed a break, as much as I did," Lisa told me with an understanding smile.

“I guess I did,” I replied. “I think I also need a break from life in general after years of being a primary caregiver for four of my family members.”

Lisa was very carefully listening to me with her eyes welling up. “You know, the main reason for our move from Boston to San Diego is that I needed a fresh start after years of being a primary caregiver for my parents,” she paused and added, “and somewhat for my aunt too.” With a quivering voice she continued, “I don’t know how you handled four people to care for and still look so amazingly put together,” she said with genuine praise.

We both felt compelled to give each other a hug. The hug lasted a long time as we both burst into tears. This process of grieving and comforting a stranger-turned-instant-friend seemed so normal. For the very first time since my mom had passed away, I cried out loud – and boy was it loud. We hugged and cried for a good fifteen minutes. It seemed that we were both taking turns wailing loudly. We ended the hugging and wailing with a bout of giggles.

“I guess grief is quite a catalyst for helping you make an instant best friend,” Lisa said to me with her face still covered in tears.

The bonding was suddenly interrupted with Lisa’s cell phone playing a James Bond theme song ringtone. “It’s my son, Mr. 007.” Lisa said with a smile.

I could feel the weight of the grief I had been carrying on my shoulders for so long shift with the good cry. I began making iced tea while Lisa took a call. When it was ready, she grabbed the glass and said "Can I bring this back? I need to rush home to handle a crisis."

From that day on, Lisa and I saw each other several times a day for a week. The following Monday, I convinced Lisa to go with me to a spa called Glen Ivy Hot Springs while the kids were back at school and our husbands were traveling. We left in the morning, right after dropping the kids off at school. We were both so excited about the idea of spending an entire day of bonding and sharing. This was our rare opportunity to unload the grief with someone whom we knew would understand. We checked into the beautiful spa with abundant natural hot water pools, saunas, hot tubs, red clay experience and yummy food. After sitting in the natural hot water pools, it was as if the pores of emotions had opened and we started sharing. I had brought my mom to this spa once and we ended up sitting in the exact spot that I had sat with my mom.

Lisa noticed my eyes welling up. "OK, Spill. What's going on?" She said in the compassionate tone of a lifelong friend.

"My mom and dad were the most loving couple I have ever met in my life. They did so much for others all their lives. I expected their old age to be filled with people going out of their way to help them. Growing up our home was like an open kitchen for all friends and family. Anyone we knew was welcome to knock on our front gate at any time of day or night and ask to be fed. To this day, I am still amazed how my mom could stock food in a way that she never ever turned anyone away. She would go into her modest kitchen and whip up delicious food. I can't begin to tell you how much they gave to others. They would take their most precious possessions and give them away to anyone that needed them, without worrying about how much it would impact their own lives. My mom was also a social butterfly and the life of a party. Her laughter was contagious. She would make jokes that were funny without being at the expense of someone else. She had an amazing sense of humor."

I talked for an hour about my parents, uncle and aunt. I shared how each caregiving experience was different and how they all impacted my life.

I touched the spot my mom had sat in the last time we had come to the spa together. I could feel sadness taking over. "Her personality was beautiful until Parkinson's stole it from her, and everyone around her." I added as tears were now streaming down my face.

As soon as I said that, I had a strong sense of not being able to speak anymore. "I can't speak anymore, your turn."

"Alright, then. Here I go. My mom and dad had been separated for over seven years. However, they both passed away within one month of each other. Dad died seven months ago and mom died six months ago, the day after my son's birthday." Lisa sighed and continued. "I could not imagine living in the house after both my mom and dad had died while we were living there. There were too many tough memories. My mom and dad did not have a very loving marriage. They had such different personalities that I always wondered how they fell in love with each other. They had almost nothing in common. My mom was outgoing and a social butterfly. She needed to be surrounded with people for her to be happy. She loved giving gifts to others. On the other hand, my dad was the happiest when he was home alone. Tinkering with his passions, collecting things and remodeling some part of the house. He had coping mechanisms over the years to put up with constant visitors at our home because of mom. He hated attending social gatherings, to the point where he even developed a low-grade fever for weeks prior to my wedding. He would have been grateful to me if I told him he didn't have to attend my wedding."

"What broke them apart was probably the starkest difference in their personalities. My mom was extremely forgiving and would never hold any grudges. Also, she had no filter. She would tell everyone whatever was on her mind without ever keeping any feelings to herself. My dad, on the other hand, had high expectations of himself and others. He would never tell anyone if their words or actions hurt him. Instead, he would bottle up all his feelings, turning them into humongous grudges for just about everyone."

Lisa continued, "When my aunt needed my mom's help, mom decided to leave my dad and move in with her. This move turned me into an instant caregiver for my dad, and to some level for my mom and aunt. My mom was the last one to pass and it was almost seven years from the day my mom moved in with my aunt. Boy, was it a roller coaster ride for those seven years!" She sighed deeply.

Lisa added, "Once my mom passed, we decided as a family that we needed a fresh start. I started looking for another job. It took me six months to find one. Fortunately, my husband could live anywhere as he travelled for his work. We decided if we were going to move from Boston, it would have to be San Diego. We were all on board with constant sunny skies and pleasant weather."

Lisa's voice began to really betray her pain. "You know, my dad killed himself while he was living with us. He overdosed on painkillers. None of us felt that we could stay in the same city, let alone the same house and recover from that kind of devastation." Her voice was soft as she was choking back tears. I knew that was enough sharing for today. We had to change the subject to move on to the rest of the day.

Over the next few weeks Lisa and I met for daily walks. Each day we found ourselves talking about a different phase of our journeys as caregivers. We would explore how it was that we had ended up becoming caregivers and what it was like to experience the end of our loved one's journeys.

I was amazed at how much we had in common. We laughed hysterically and cried violently from the depths our souls. It was so powerful to have someone listen to me so emphatically and to be able to share my grief with a person who understood and knew what it was like to walk in my shoes. I know Lisa felt the same way.

It really felt as if we were taking a load off each other's back every time we met. I would come home feeling so much lighter. My husband said to me, "It is great to see you smile more." Lisa's husband and kids were delighted to have more home cooked meals again.

Three months later, I got an opportunity to go on a camping trip with my daughter. It was meant to be a great bonding experience for the two of us.

The first day of the camp, I found myself greatly missing my supportive conversations with my new friend Lisa. After lunch, an energetic and flamboyant thirty-year-old camp counselor informed the kids, "Tomorrow morning I want you all to tell stories about a difficult time in your life and what you did to overcome it. I want you all to understand it is easier to learn from someone else's experiences rather than have to go through that same difficult experience yourself." He added, "When the person with the experience shares their story, they are giving a huge gift to the listeners."

He ended the session by saying something that hit me straight in the heart: "A life experience not shared with others is not worth having."

That night I tossed and turned partly because the mattress was uncomfortable, but mainly because I was trying to figure out what was the best way for me to tell my story to others. I was restless, and got up in the middle of a star-filled night, and as I was walking it dawned on me why I was attending this camp. I needed this morning's experience to realize that Lisa and I had important stories to tell that would help other caregivers in their journey.

"I need to write this book," I said out loud looking up at the stars.

When I got back to my tent, I took my phone out and texted Lisa telling her my thoughts and asking her permission to write this book that encompassed both our experiences. A minute after I sent the email, I got a reply with a resounding "YES! GREAT IDEA!"

Lisa texted, "I recall your mom hated being labeled a senior. In her honor, I think we should use the word seenager in this book."

Her next text message was, " Seenager: someone who has seen a lot in life and is aging. A senior teenager who finally has everything they desired in their TEEN years; no school, a monthly income without working, savings to spend on whatever, driver's license even with bad driving, no curfew, no acne, access to legal drugs, and above all (gasp!) sex without fear of pregnancy."

I responded with a "LOL! That sounds great!"

Her last text message that night was "Last but not the least, and actually my favorite similarity is: the age excused emotional outbursts."

I responded with: "My favorite too, we certainly have seen a lot of that. LOL!"

My last text that night was "I better get in a few Zzzs tonight if I want to avoid emotional outbursts tomorrow when we have to go for a long and steep hike. Good night!"

The request to use seenager instead of senior from Lisa made me feel that she had not just closely listened to my stories, but she had truly embraced them as her own.

Luckily, I had decided to bring my laptop and an extended charger on the camping trip with me. For the next six days, I recharged whenever we would go to the dining hall at night. During the day, there was little to no Internet, so all I could do on my laptop was write. I would sit in various spots around the campground and write. I had been instructed to avoid being a helicopter parent, hovering over my child. So, I kept my distance and sat behind trees where I could still see my daughter but she could not see me.

Chapter 2 – Starting Our Caregiving Journeys

We Were Least Prepared for the Caregiver Role

I was thrown into a caregiver role, mostly at times when my plate was already full and I did not think I could add anything else to it. Sometimes I became a caregiver to deal with a loved one's acute health crisis, while at other times, it was because their chronic health condition was reaching a new low.

I was in denial for years about being a caregiver, even though I was calling my parents every night to check how their day went. My parents certainly were in denial about my role as their caregiver as well. The reality was that they did not want to take my advice about the many details of everyday life including moving, seeing a doctor or eating an appropriate diet, just to name a few.

My performance as a caregiver was not consistent and my focus on what I did for my seenagers was different depending on their needs and on my availability and capability.

Once significant life-changing events happened, I had no choice but to accept that I was a caregiver; and neither did Lisa.

Reflecting on the life journey of the people we were as caregivers is amazing, inspiring and tough all at the same time.

In this chapter, we will introduce our seenagers and why we took on the caregiver role for them.

Emotionally Absent Caregiver

Alli – My Aunt

I regret to this day being an emotionally absent caregiver for my aunt. It would have taken probably an hour out of my life to meet her emotional needs.

Child: Aunt Alli was a happy and beautiful child that got a lot of love and attention from her parents and extended family.

Teenager: She was a smart, intelligent, vibrant and happy teenager, who was good at studies and popular in school.

Adult: Aunt Alli got married to a very successful businessman and had two children. She was a housewife and was well respected by everyone who knew her. She lost her oldest son to a car accident and then became clinically depressed. Her husband left her, took the other child with him and moved to another country.

Seenager: She was lonely, sad and depressed. She had money to take care of herself, and lived on her own. Occasionally traveled to see her siblings, who were never very happy about her visit.

Care Recipient: I became her caregiver and stayed for a few weeks in the hospital with her at the end of her life when she was diagnosed with cancer at the age of eighty-one.

I was visiting my parents in Pakistan in 2002, at the same time my aunt came over from India for a visit. She had not seen my dad since he had left India in 1965. On the second day of my visit, my aunt experienced a very severe episode of what we perceived to be an asthma attack. She was gasping for breath, so I called an ambulance. They took her to the hospital where she was diagnosed with stage four breast cancer that had metastasized to her lungs.

"Did you ever notice a lump in your breast?" I asked my aunt before she died.

"Yes, I had noticed one recently," she answered.

I wanted to ask her why she had not gone to see a doctor but I was afraid that my aunt would be brutally honest and tell me that she had not gone simply because she wanted to die.

Knowing too well first hand that if breast cancer was detected in its early stages it has a very high survival rate, it was really hard to see my aunt suffering.

My visit with my parents turned into a caregiving visit for my aunt. My planned short visit turned into a full month. During the visit, I took planned business trips to Singapore and Taiwan. I did not have very strong emotional ties with my aunt, as I was meeting her for the first time in my life.

Given that the whole purpose of my trip was to take care of things for my parents and I was working at night (while it was day in the USA), I barely had enough time during the day to take care of my aunt's practical needs. I was there for discussions with her doctors, paying bills, getting things scheduled for her, and following up on her day-to-day needs. However, neither did I have the time, nor the energy to deal with my aunt's emotional needs.

Never did I have a conversation with her about her fears and desires. I regret it to this day. I went on a couple more week-long trips to Pakistan to be an advocate for her in her healthcare. This was my shortest experience as a caregiver and certainly the most unexpected one.

The memory of my aunt looking in my eyes with an appreciative smile and squeezing my hand tightly is a treasured memory now.

She wanted to make sure I realized how much my presence meant to her and how much she appreciated what I was doing for her.

I do feel badly however about getting anxious every time she would squeeze my hand for what felt like an hour-long squeeze. I felt that she was wasting the limited time I had. I felt resentful because sitting idly with her longer meant I could not do the fifty other things I had on my plate for the day. My impatience with her prevented me from being able to fully experience her love for me, and enjoying the rare smiles that were there only for my benefit.

Physically Absent Caregiver

Sami – My Uncle

From time to time I would turn into a Physically Absent Caregiver for a few weeks as a coping mechanism, during his impossible tirades.

Child: *Uncle Sami was a very spoiled only child. He was quick to throw temper tantrums when he did not get his way.*

Teenager: *As a teenager, he was book smart but had low emotional intelligence. He did well in school and got admitted at UC Berkley School of Engineering.*

Adult: *He graduated at the top of his engineering class then decided to get his MBA. He started a technology company with a friend. His role at the company was Chief Financial Officer. He was instrumental in getting the company sold for big profits at the age of 55. He married a woman with a daughter from her previous marriage. She died of cancer seven years after they married. He never remarried or even dated much after that.*

Seenager: *He was a loner after he retired. He had a few hobbies and liked going to bars and restaurants by himself.*

Care Recipient: I became his caregiver a few years after he retired. His diabetes was getting worse, as was his drinking. He was finally diagnosed with prostate cancer.

My uncle could be very difficult to talk to – he repeated himself, got angry, complained and was verbally abusive, especially when he was drunk. I was really the only person in his life that could possibly become his primary caregiver. We had frequent conversations that went like this: "Do you recall the time when your mom was stuck in London because she missed her connecting flight and I made special flight arrangements for her to get to the USA so she could attend your cousins' wedding?"

I would respond with a deep sigh and a big smile on my face, knowing full well what was coming next. "Yes, I do Uncle."

He would respond brimming with pride. "I had to call so many airlines and be on hold for hours before I could get someone to help me. I had to pay an extra $100 for the ticket to get that all setup for your mom."

I would respond, "Yes, that was really great of you." He would then follow up with, "So I know you will take good care of me when I cannot do that for myself."

It was as if he wanted to cash in his chips for all the good things he had done for others.

I felt very ill-prepared to care for him. He had a unique way of getting under my skin and making me feel obligated and guilty. For example, he constantly had small requests like calling the phone company for him. These seemingly small tasks were actually quite time-consuming. I already had so little available time as it was.

When my personal life was extra busy, I felt I neither had time nor energy to take his calls. Sometimes, guilty feelings would wake me up in the middle of the night leading me to call him back the next day. A couple of times he called me while I was travelling and dealing with severe issues with my parents. When I did not return his call, he had his friend call me. I felt it was very demanding and insensitive of him to do that, since he just wanted attention and someone to talk to.

I knew that my uncle would notice my state of stress every time and follow up with "I just got two tickets for us to see a show." He and I enjoyed stand-up comedians. He used to attend all the shows of one of his few close friends, who had been a very successful stand-up comedian. I always enjoyed the shows with him, even when the stand-up comedian was not very funny. My uncle would find the hidden gems of humor in the acts, and do a very big belly laugh. His laugh would always crack me up.

Before every conversation with my uncle I would promise myself that I was going to be very patient with him, because I did feel a lot of empathy for his situation. I would promise myself I would behave at least this one time. Inevitably I could not control my emotional outbursts in the face of his highly unreasonable behavior. The worst incident happened when I was in the hospital with my dad. My mom was not feeling well that day either. My uncle called ten times in thirty minutes. I could not take his call as I was waiting for dad's doctor to call me. When I finally called him back, he said, "I hope your parents are doing well today. I was trying to send a picture of the stream behind my backyard that is flooded due to heavy rain, and the camera that you got for me is not focusing very well when I zoom in."

I had an outburst that I still regret to this day. "You are the most selfish person I know. It is insane that you are calling me incessantly with no regard to what is going on in our lives. Please don't call me again." A few months later, after many rounds of apologies and with assurances that I wanted to take care of him, he forgave me.

My uncle finally deteriorated to a point where he could no longer take care of himself. I had no choice but to step in to help him. I was totally overwhelmed and felt the weight of the world on my shoulders.

Caregiver for Someone Who Takes Charge

Jay– My Dad

In some ways, it was easier to be a caregiver for someone who took charge of their own care. However, when he was stubborn it would be very difficult to convince him to do what was needed.

Child: My dad was known for his kind and loving nature as a child. He won everyone's heart with his hugs and smiles.

Teenager: As a teenager, his only focus was studying. He went to a public university and got good grades.

Adult: He married the girl next door. He hated to socialize, and was always worrying either about his work or about his family. He was a workaholic and grew through the ranks of a successful non-profit company. He finally retired at age sixty-five as the CEO of the company.

Seenager: After he retired he became a full-time caregiver for his wife who had Parkinson's disease. He smoked a lot while he was working, but quit when he retired. He suffered from COPD due to his chain smoking and had a weak heart.

Care Recipient: Overtime I took on more and more of a caregiver role for him. However, I became his primary caregiver when he was struggling to take care of both himself and mom.

My dad was a take-charge kind of guy. He understood his body and the challenges he had with it all too well. He was constantly on the Internet searching for information about his health issues, medications, home remedies, energy healing, homeopathy and a lot more.

He was both in tune with his body and a worrywart at the same time. This was not a very good combination. I don't know how many times we had the following conversation:

Dad: "I have not had a bowel movement for two days."

Me: "What should we do? Should I call the doctor?"

Dad: "Not yet, but I am worried. I have already taken all the herbal medications, I have done all the acupressure points. I finally took some Pepto Bismol a few hours ago."

I inwardly cringed, knowing that was not the right medication for his symptoms. It was a constant worry of mine that he would take the wrong medication.

Me: "I am so sorry to hear that. Wait a little while and try Ex-Lax instead. I will check in with you in a few hours to see if you want me to do something for you."

I learned over the years that telling him not to worry, suggesting things for him to try, and getting upset with him for his obsessive worrying about his body, was just going to make things worse. I learned that what helped most was simply listening to him describe the situation fully, empathizing with him, and then offering to help. In the end, this is what he needed from me.

We had always wondered if my dad would be able to retire, as he could not sit still. If he was not working long hours at work, he was busy helping some family member or doing things for his community. However, his calling after retirement became taking care of his beloved wife. To see him cook, clean, help mom put on her clothes, bathe her and pray with her was not something I would have ever believed could happen, if I had not seen it with my own eyes.

He kept my mom's condition as hidden from me as he could. After he died and I got to see first-hand what my mom was going through, I understood why every night he would take a shot of bourbon and sit on his laptop until the wee hours of the morning with his headset on. When anyone would give him advice, he would just recite this verse of a poem:

It's no longer a friendship when friends turn into instructors

True friends carry you through difficult times

and become compassionate listeners

He would give 1000 percent to anything he did in his life. It is a lot more heartbreaking now for me to reflect back on the sharp contrast of his professional life to his retired life. My dad worked as the CEO of a prestigious non-profit with almost 10,000 employees worldwide. He was so well respected that no one would have dared to say anything to offend him. It wasn't that he was a dictator, but his leadership style commanded respect from every level of his organization. Even now after so many years when I meet someone that used to work for him, I can see such reverence and respect for him.

My dad had the kindest eyes. When he looked at me with his dad eyes, I always felt like his princess that could never do anything wrong. He made me feel like I was perfect. Whenever I felt like I messed up something in life, I had to just call him or go see him. He would appreciate me with all my flaws.

When my dad was hospitalized, my hands were very full taking care of him and mom, along with lots of other responsibilities. I'll never forget the day I entered my dad's hospital as my phone was ringing. There was a crisis at work. I had to leave his room. While I was taking care of the crisis at work, I got a text message from my daughter. She needed to be picked up from soccer practice. Then a text message came from my husband that the garage door was not opening and he did not have the keys to get in the house. Three hours later I got back to my dad only to find him fast asleep. It was a Friday afternoon and the doctor was now long gone leaving me with tons of unanswered questions. The social worker was also gone until Monday.

The year that he was too sick to oversee his own care and I had to step in was one of the hardest years of my life. I constantly felt I was dropping balls and not getting to important meetings on time. I was also gaining weight, sleeping poorly and as a whole, felt like a complete mess. The worst part of it all was that this deep level of stress and feelings of being a failure prevented me from seeing myself through his warm loving eyes as his perfect princess.

Best Physical Intention Caregiver

Ruby – My Mom

I always interacted with the best physical intentions as a caregiver, but I still did not feel I was doing enough.

Child: *My mom was a joyful child with a naughty streak. She was the youngest of eight kids, and loved to get in trouble.*

Teenager: *As a teenager, her goal was to have fun. She had a lot of friends and was definitely the leader of the popular kids.*

Adult: *My parents married young and she had me before their first anniversary. Her life was filled with attending social gatherings and traveling, with or without dad. Dad did all the worrying for both of them, and mom enjoyed life.*

Seenager: *My mother was diagnosed with Parkinson's disease at the age of sixty. By age sixty-five, she needed full-time care. Her primary symptom was tremors, but as the years went on, we started seeing a lot of other symptoms. These included drug induced dementia, rigidity, speech changes, nightmares, falling, trouble swallowing, etc. My dad was the primary caregiver for mom for twenty years.*

Care Recipient: I became her primary caregiver when my dad was not able to any longer. Even though I was somewhat involved as his backup caregiver for mom, it was quite shocking to experience first-hand all that he had been doing for her.

She was just not the same person. She used to make these faces that were so painful to watch while she slept. It used to feel like someone was torturing her, but there was nothing I could do to save her. Trying to wake her from the nightmares worked occasionally. In the last few months of her life she would scream in pain with tortured facial expressions, and then there was absolutely nothing we could do to wake her up. It was like seeing your mom being tormented in the most horrific way, without knowing how or who was doing it, and having no way to stop it. I wouldn't wish that fate on my worst enemy.

Of all the caregivers, I have seen or heard about, I would say that my dad deserves the "Best Caregiver" award. When he died and I had to fill his big shoes as a caregiver for my mom, it was very overwhelming.

A year before he retired, my mom was diagnosed with Parkinson's disease. The day he retired, he decided to devote himself as a full-time caregiver for his wife. My biggest argument with him was, "you treat mom like Queen Bee, and do everything for her. Please at least let her get her own water and take her own meds." He took over all of my mom's chores around the house and became her medical advocate, her crutch and her cheerleader.

People around my parents would say how lucky my mom was to have a husband who was such a perfect caregiver. Over the years as my mom's condition got worse, so did my dad's. However, the roles and responsibilities did not change. In the last few hours of his life while he was on hospice care, he was worried about my mom's medications. As my mom started to get sleepy sitting in a chair by his bedside, he asked if we could get a roll-away bed in his hospital room so she could lie down. The entire family was shocked when he died before her. We never expected that, and I did not have a true appreciation for all that he had been doing for my mom until I had to fill in for him.

My mom moved in with me when my father passed away. I did not realize how little time I was spending with her until one day she said to me, "Can you just sit down with me for a few minutes and talk today?" Her room was right next to the garage. As mom slept almost all day and would get up at all odd hours, we needed someone with her twenty-four hours a day. She needed meds and food at specific times, as well as help getting in and out of bed. For two months after my dad's passing, I tried to see if I could get her on a schedule. I tried to make her life more structured by getting a caregiver to come for a few hours a day rather than be there all day waiting for her to wake up. But I failed miserably at the goal of bringing structure into her life.

After two months, I had to go back to work and it was evident that we needed to find someone to provide her with round-the-clock-care. I found a mother-daughter caregiver team so that my time with her was spent on brief check-ins with her as well as with her new team so that I could assist them with their daily needs. This allowed me to ensure that her medical needs were met, and that she was safe with appropriate food available for her in the house.

There were days that I could sit down with mom and just do idle chit-chat. She would tell me stories from her past that were definitely very naughty. We had some good laughs about her travels, where she did things that my dad would certainly not have approved, like going to a foreign country without a visa, going on a "cheap African lion safari" where the lion had been allowed to come close enough for her to touch. She would tell these stories with a twinkle in her eyes, giggling as she narrated the naughtiest parts of the story.

On most days, I would rush in and out of her room on my way to and from work. Farming out the most time-consuming tasks enabled me to focus on my job and family responsibilities. However, I still was the primary caregiver with a high level of oversight and decision-making for my mom's care.

An Instant Caregiver – Domino Effect

For Lisa's Aunt (Mariya), Mom (Aliya) and Dad (Noah)

Aunt Mariya's need created a domino effect that made Lisa an instant caregiver for her aunt, mom and dad.

Lisa's plate was already full with two kids, an executive level corporate job, and a husband that travelled a lot for his. This was no time in her life to add anything else, but ready or not, here she was with added responsibilities for her parents and her aunt.

Mariya - Lisa's Aunt

Child: Aunt Mariya was a quiet child, with occasional temper tantrums. She did not have a lot of friends. She had two best friends, and one sibling.

Teenager: She was an average student and graduated from college with a finance degree.

Adult: She got married right after college and had a son. She divorced her first husband because he was abusive. She worked as an accountant for a small company. She remarried ten years later and was widowed after seven years.

Seenager: She was strong-willed. Right after she retired at the age of sixty-seven, she started showing signs of memory loss. A year later she was diagnosed with Alzheimer's disease.

Care Recipient: Lisa became Aunt Mariya's caregiver when Lisa's mom decided to get involved in Aunt Mariya's caregiving needs. Since Lisa's mom was not always able to deal with her aunt's needs, Lisa would get sucked into the situation to help her mom take care of Aunt Mariya's needs.

Noah - Lisa's Dad

Child: Lisa's dad was an angry child. He had ADHD and was very impatient with everyone around him. He wanted things his way.

Teenager: His parents hired someone to help him with his schoolwork. He got interested in engineering and his passion for science helped him get more focused in his studies as he grew older.

Adult: He fell in love with Lisa's mom when he worked on a project with her at work. He followed her until she said yes. 'Opposites attract' was certainly the theme of their marriage. He worked for several companies and progressed well in his career. He got his way, both at work and at home.

Seenager: He suffered from rheumatoid arthritis of the knees, right after he turned fifty. Also, one month after Lisa's mom moved in with her aunt Mariya, he was in a big car accident. After that, he started complaining about severe pain all over his body and got depressed. He was eventually diagnosed with fibromyalgia.

Care Recipient: Lisa became his caregiver soon after her mom moved in with aunt Mariya, as her parents practically separated after that.

Aliya - Lisa's Mom

Child: Aliya was a happy and beautiful child who thrived on being the center of attention. She would play with anyone, no matter how old or young they were.

Teenager: Her school years were focused on making friends. She would hang out with kids ranging from the most popular kids to a lonely new kid.

Adult: She graduated with a degree in marketing. She got a job at a Fortune 100 company and worked there her entire career. She got married at the age of twenty-seven and had three kids. She was a social butterfly.

Seenager: She needed people around her. She was a breast cancer survivor. Even when she was in pain, she would not want to stay home, feeling that socializing kept her young.

Care Recipient: Lisa became her caregiver when she moved in with her Aunt, because issues that her dad took care of for her mom were now on Lisa's shoulders. When her father died, her mom moved in with her. Even though she was experiencing chest pain for a couple of months, she was not one to complain, so her health issues remained undiagnosed.

At 8:00 am one morning when Lisa was getting ready to take her kids to school, and get on a conference call at the same time, she started getting calls from her mom and text messages from her dad. "We need to talk now," texted her dad three times in one hour.

Over the years, her parents' relationship had deteriorated and she had feared that one day they may want to get a divorce. There was something in these short five words that made her heart skip a beat, as she feared the worst. Even though her parents fought a lot, they always came back together.

She kept saying a prayer as she picked up the phone and called her dad. Her dad told her "Everything came to a head last night when Aunt Mariya called mom in a panic." Lisa understood very well that since her dad did not like Aunt Mariya or her kids, he had put his foot down and said, "If you go to visit your sister, I will divorce you." Aunt Mariya was now frail, had Alzheimer's disease and she lived with her son and daughter-in-law. In her younger days, she was bubbly, vivacious and did not have a filter. What she thought came out of her mouth without regard for how the listener would take it.

After listening to her dad's side of the story, she called her mom who told her that her aunt Mariya's daughter-in-law had hired a new caregiver for her six months ago. She had a sense of urgency in her voice. She went on to explain that Aunt Mariya had called her again yesterday to say that the caregiver beat and pushed her all the time, and that her own son did not believe her.

Lisa questioned her mom and told her that although she really loved Aunt Mariya, she was not always someone who was in touch with reality.

"She has called me multiple times complaining about it. However, last night she was crying. She has not cried in years. Honey, I have to go and check this out for myself. I will never be able to live with myself if I don't," Lisa's mom replied with a sigh.

"I am going to fly in today so that we can talk about this in person. Can you please hold off for a day?" Lisa told her mom.

As soon as she hung up the phone, Lisa started making her plans. She went to work to cancel all her meetings for the next two weeks, and planned how she was going to handle critical projects remotely. She called in favors from all her friends in the neighborhood, kissed her family goodbye and was on a plane to see her parents by 5 pm that night.

When Lisa got to her parent's home at 8:00 pm that night, they both wanted to talk to her first. By midnight they both had a chance to plead their cases in Lisa's court.

Lisa convinced her mom that night to let her step in and help. "I will go visit Aunt Mariya and see if what she was telling her is true."

The very next morning at 8 am Lisa called Aunt Mariya and told her, "I am coming to see you today. I will be there by 1 pm."

Aunt Mariya responded with extreme excitement, "Oh dear Lisa, I can't wait to see you. I just talked to your mom last night. Are you bringing your mom with you too?"

Lisa responded with a calming voice, "No, not today, but I can't wait to see you."

By 8:30 am Lisa started a four-hour drive to Kansas City. She knew that Aunt Mariya's son would be upset that she was going there unannounced. Even though Aunt Mariya had a backyard cottage, it was only a hundred feet from his home.

Aunt Mariya did not want her family to know Lisa was on her way to visit. Unfortunately, the caregiver overheard the conversation and told her daughter-in-law Anna. Anna texted Lisa by 10:33 am "We do not want you to interfere in our family's affairs and you are not welcome to visit our home or Aunt Mariya."

Lisa had just taken an exit in the college town of Columbia, Missouri and stopped at a coffee shop when she saw the text. Lisa called her brother's friend John who lived in Columbia and asked him, “I have a really huge favor to ask you. Can I come over to your office now and explain?” He had always been such a wonderful and caring man. She was hoping that he was not busy that day.

After Lisa was done confiding in him, she felt like she had to add, “Please do not share any of this with anyone, can you please promise me?” He replied with a warm smile, “You know you can count on me.”

By 4 pm that day, John was able to bring Aunt Mariya out of her home to meet Lisa at a famous KC Steak House. This spot used to be Aunt Mariya and Uncle Tom’s favorite date nightspot. She was so happy to see Lisa. They hugged and talked, laughed and cried.

Aunt Mariya took her to the restroom and showed her the bruises on her arm from the abuse she had endured from the caregiver. Lisa was in a state of shock. She could not imagine how her cousin would let something like this happen to his own mom. He traveled so much for his job and was hardly around, but still Lisa felt that this was no excuse.

Holding back tears, she told Aunt Mariya, “I will have mom visit you very soon. Let me go back to mom’s home tonight and we will let you know when she is going to come over.” No sooner had those words come out of her mouth that a sinking feeling set in her body. The domino effect of that decision was going to completely change

Lisa's own life too. She was going to become a caregiver for her emotionally and physically demanding dad, while her mother was going to become Aunt Mariya's caregiver.

Soon after, Lisa realized that she was not only a caregiver for her dad, but also for her mom and a proxy caregiver for her Aunt Mariya as well.

Summary

There were times I would deny that I was a caregiver. I was afraid that I would rate myself a failure if I admitted that I was caring for a grown adult who was vulnerable and dependent on me for both small and big decisions in life. The challenges of being a caregiver were tremendous. There were countless balls I had to juggle in my life, including professional responsibilities and the things I wanted or had to do for my husband, kids and home.

I was also responsible for the health and well-being of a full-grown adult. I often felt like a complete failure because I could not, in all possible scenarios, meet all the demands in my life all at once. I would often get somewhere late or let someone down both at work and in my personal life.

I grew up with lots of friends and family around me. Even though I grew up in an urban city during my childhood, it had all the makings of an old-fashioned village. In my village, people were meddlesome, something which annoyed me a lot as a child, but that I missed as an adult caregiver. I needed them now to be in my business and help me take care of my parents, aunt and uncle. Losing this sense of closeness and community was the first big loss (of many) I experienced in my journey as a caregiver.

The most traumatic thing about the care-giving role was watching people I loved deteriorate physically, mentally and emotionally.

On the other hand, being the primary caregiver gave me an opportunity to express love and get closure. In hindsight, I would definitely volunteer again to be their primary caregiver.

Chapter 3 – Arguments All Around

Clouds Were Inevitable but So Was Sunshine

I was lucky to have a wonderful relationship with my parents. But even such great relationships became strained at times when the physical and mental health of my parents changed, or the time and energy demands placed on me as their caregiver become unmanageable.

Interestingly, the contentious relationship with my uncle improved as I became his caregiver. His antagonistic behavior taught me how to not take his hostility personally. In actuality, he treated everyone and every idea with firm opposition. Once I became his caregiver, his dependence on me rendered him humble and grateful. I was grateful for the change in our relationship.

Our relationships with our respective seenagers changed over time, improving or worsening, depending on what was going on. Knowing that we could not change or control the behavior of our seenagers went a long way in making our caregiving journeys easier.

Also, it helped with peace of mind not to take things too personally. We laughed about the fact that not only was the word "No" used most frequently by our seenagers, it was also the word we heard most from our kids. We both agreed it was far easier to deal with a kid's "No" even when they were teenagers, than it was to deal with a seenager's "No."

Lisa and I reminisced about these contentious topics. We found some of the most combative discussions in our respective journeys caring for our seenagers to be hysterically funny in hindsight. Others yet, were still to raw and source of tremendous grief.

Garage Standard Time - GST

Jay

My solution to arguments about leaving home on time.

Arriving on time became a real issue when my caregiving responsibilities started to include transportation and case management with clinicians. No matter what I tried, my dad was never ready on time. Now that my parents were living with us, this became a sore subject and a point of contention between us. I was responsible for taking him to his doctor's appointments but I was at a loss as to how to get him to be ready on time. During this time, I often worked from home. I would come down after a conference call, ready to take him to the doctor's office, only to find that he was still in the process of getting ready and nowhere near ready to leave the house. We finally agreed on what we called "Garage Standard Time." This is the time my dad had to be ready and meet me in the garage with the inhaler in his pocket and shoes on.

"Dad we have to leave at 10:00 am GST for your appointment with the pulmonologist." I would remind him in the morning. After months of arguing over punctuality, we were both ready for a truce and this solution worked for us.

Spending vs. Saving

Jay & Sami

I don't know who is more difficult to deal with, someone who saves every penny or someone spends on everyone else and doesn't worry about their future.

As one approaches the end of life, living, caregiving and health expenses can really add up. My dad certainly had not planned for this.

My dad and uncle could not have been more polar opposites. My uncle saved every penny for his future, while my dad used every penny possible to help others.

My uncle was very stingy with his money. There came a time when my uncle could not do much around the house by himself. Consequently, the condition of his home deteriorated exponentially. Some days it was hard for anyone to go into his home and tolerate the foul smells. His priority was to save as much money as he possibly could until the very end of his life. His only purpose was watching sports alone at home with his beer.

My dad, on the other hand, spent all of his money in helping others and my mom gave away all of her jewelry as presents. Nothing gave them more joy than helping others. Later in life when they didn't have any more physical things to give away, they became a prayer service and a home remedy hotline for their friends and family. My parents rarely watched TV and never watched sports. Both of them liked to read or help others.

Things did change with my dad at the tail end of his life, when reality sunk in that he and mom would outlast the very small nest egg he had.

One day, my dad forced me to sit down with him to have a very "serious conversation." This was the first time I saw a real sense of panic in his voice about money.

"Rosie, I am very sorry that we have had to rely on you for money many a times in our lives. I feel really ashamed about that," my father said.

My heart was bleeding as I heard the desperation in my proud and very accomplished dad's voice.

"What if one of us ends up needing professional caregivers or has to be moved into memory care? My friend just told me how expensive that is. I am really concerned about that," he added with tears in his eyes.

All I could do at that time was to stay calm, look at him with love and tell him "Dad, please do not to worry. I have thought about this already. We had a family meeting and talked about how we can all chip in, plus there are non-profits and other resources I have found in San Diego that will be able to help."

Unlike other topics we discussed "seriously," he did not pressure me to provide any detail. He probably could sense some trepidation in my voice and he did not want to see me upset. I saw him praying for a long time that night. I knew what was on top of the prayer list and it truly made me sad to know that he was worried about being a financial burden for me.

At the end of the day it all worked out okay for my dad. I guess I didn't need to plead with him not to let mom spend money on big money gifts to family and friends. His response would always be "that makes her feel good. Let her." I guess with all the good they did in the world, they left the world a much better place.

My uncle, on the other hand, saved a lot of money for his rainy days. I suspected that he was hoarding money rather than use it to make his own life comfortable. Over the years, I argued with my uncle to get a cleaning service to keep his home clean, "That is not worth my money, I can do that myself." He left a lot of money unused at the end of his life.

Repeating Stories vs. Expecting Me to Know

Jay & Sami

I felt that both of these experiences were designed to develop my patience.

On days that I had a lot on my plate, my patience would run very thin when my dad would start describing his health ailments and challenges for the day in painstaking details. He would repeat himself and talk very slowly. Whenever he noticed my frustration, he would withdraw and say, “It’s okay, I am fine.” That would make me more frustrated since now I had to spend time convincing him I really wanted to know what was going on with him. This would take a while, and if I were able to convince him, he would start the story of the day all over again.

I learned over time to not be impatient when he was telling a story. If I was in a rush I would quickly summarize what I had heard thus far and add, “I really want to hear the rest of it. I will take time tonight to talk. I love you. See you soon.”

On the other hand, my uncle would expect me to understand what was going on with him after he shared the tiniest information. If I tried to get more detail from him, he would get angry.

One time he called me as I was on my way home from work. He said, “I am out of anything for breakfast.” I asked patiently, “I am going to stop by Costco, what can I bring for you?” After a brief pause, I added, “Could you just text me what you want?” His curt response was: “You should know.”

I felt I was foolish enough to continue the discussion by saying “I just don’t want to forget anything you may need and I don’t know if you have any special things you feel like eating today.” He started his long tirade: “You have bought breakfast food for me many times. You know the milk is always 2%. Even though I have warned you so many times not to buy organic, you keep doing that. The organic food lobby is just a way for these big corporations to rob money from poor people who don’t know any better…”

He talked non-stop for five minutes, complaining about all kinds of things, including how I did not pay attention. He then started to add “I have told you many times...” I just could not listen to that anymore. I hung up on him and turned off my phone. I bought what I could think of for him. When I got to his home to deliver the food, I used my keys to get in, put the groceries inside his front door, while yelling out loud so he could hear me over the TV, “I have to run. I am putting the food here. My phone is out of battery.” I closed the front door and drove away fast, before he could stop me.

I felt bad about treating him in that manner, but I felt justified in doing what I did because of the way he treated me. I felt that was not the best coping mechanism, but the only one I had energy for that day. I did eventually convince him to order his groceries online from the local grocery store by saying, “You know you can order what you need, not have to throw away food and save money.” He finally agreed to do that.

You Never Have Time for Me

Ruby, Jay & Sami

I wish the role of caregiver came with extra hours in the day.

I probably never wished more fervently to have more hours in the day than when I was a caregiver. The one thing my loved ones needed most from me was the gift of my ability to spend more time with them. During those days as a caregiver, I often felt that I never had enough time to give to my demanding seenagers – and they often shared this sentiment.

Even when my parents lived with me, I constantly heard them say: "Can we just sit and talk? You never have time for us, you are always in a rush."

My aunt's complaint was: "you never call." Which was actually true. I never made time to call her before I became her caregiver for a short period of time.

My uncle who lived in the same city was insulin-dependent and hated to take shots by himself. So, every time I visited him, he would ask me to extend my stay.

"Can you give me my injection today, you know how much I hate doing it for myself?" He would often ask me.

The truth is that I was squeamish about needles and did not like giving shots at all. But I did not have the heart to refuse him. Without fail, I would push myself to do it. I hate to admit this but sometimes I would whisper under my breath, "You jerk, trying to squeeze out every last drop of time I have."

Extended Family Chaos

Ruby, Jay, Sami

Any reasonable person can go crazy with the many opinions, varying approaches, differing priorities and dysfunctional relationships.

I argued with my seenagers as well regarding the chaos the extended family was creating on a regular basis. Every week there was a new crisis in one of their lives because of something a family member said or did. Some of the family members ended up on my "blacklist." Once someone got on the blacklist I just did not want to have my seenagers tell me anything about that family member. The list started with one person but grew over time.

I had a blacklist for my uncle too. At the top of that list was his stepdaughter who would constantly advise my uncle to buy something new. Every time she suggested something for my uncle to buy or do, he would get into analysis paralysis and want to discuss the pros and cons repeatedly. He was into gadgets and so was she.

My uncle needed a good cleaning service to keep his home clean, his clothes and dishes washed and put away. Everything needed to be picked up and put in a proper place that he could find later. When my uncle talked about his frustration of not being able to keep his home clean, his stepdaughter suggested he buy Roomba (the vacuuming robot). Feeling that it was too expensive, he decided against it. However, every time I talked to him for a month after that, he would second-guess his decision and say, “Do you think I should buy it?” Inevitably, before I would have a chance to answer his questions he would make comments like “the mechanics of the robot are iffy. I am not sure how well it will do on the corners and under the furniture…”

One day finally my irritation level reached an all-time high. I let myself cool down for a day, then the next day, I went to his house. I asked him to walk with me as I picked up clothes, dishes, papers and empty bottles from the floor, counters, closet, etc. The entire time I was doing this, I said, “a Roomba cannot pick this up.” When I thought he was finally getting my drift, I said “Only Rosie or someone she can send to your home daily can do that for you. Will you please let me find someone?”

I learned a private mantra to keep me calm, with pictures of extended family members in my head: “They don’t know because they are not here.” I would take a breath in, and exhaling, I would add out loud, “Let Go.”

What to Eat and What Not to Eat

Ruby & Sami

Keeping up with what, how much, and when someone eats is a challenge with a baby, but can be a nightmare with a seenager.

I thought dealing with my daughter who was a picky eater was hard. It was ten times more difficult having conversations about food with my mom and uncle while trying to keep them marginally well nourished.

I found myself arguing over the amount, frequency and type of food my mom was supposed to eat every time I talked to her. No matter how much she was served she would say "This is way too much, I can't possibly eat that much." If we gave her a glass of Glucerna (a nutritional shake for people with diabetes) she would drink it and refuse to eat anything else for the day. Anytime I would try to talk to her about her eating habits she would get the naughtiest smile and turn away from me. Then without looking into my eyes she would say, "I just cannot hear you."

On the other hand, my diabetic uncle ate too much or ate foods dangerous for him. He was insulin-dependent and would often tell me, “I took my shot for the day so I can eat a scoop of ice cream,” or worse yet, “I took a double dose of insulin today because I ate two scoops of ice cream.” His doctor had explained to him many times that was not good logic. It drove me crazy, as his health would generally worsen as a result of his illogical actions.

Absurd Opinions

Sami

Arguing became a sport for my uncle. He always had to win. Arguing also became a way to prolong every interaction we had.

I have often said, "I beg to differ…" or "I see the situation differently…" when speaking to friends, family and colleagues. I must say however that my uncle's failing judgment had me telling him "you are wrong" way too frequently. He could be so hot tempered and would frequently get into arguments with people. He often felt that he was in the right and that everyone around him was wrong.

My uncle would argue over the most ridiculous things, including the weather. If I was taking him out somewhere and asked him to wear a jacket because it was cold outside, he would start arguing about how the weatherman is an idiot.

"Who needs a jacket in September after the level of global warming we are experiencing." I learned overtime to not even ask him to keep a jacket, rather I would keep his jacket in my car without him looking. One time when we were at a doctor's office and he said, “Boy, I wonder why they always keep their office so cold?” I went to the car and got his jacket.

“How did you have my jacket with you?” he asked. I responded, “I picked it up just in case you got cold.”

Coping Mechanism

Ruby & Jay

My mom dealt with tough symptoms of Parkinson's disease with a sense of humor, my dad with alcohol.

My dad was my mom's primary caregiver for nearly twenty years. Over the years, as her Parkinson's disease and dementia grew worse her personality kept changing for the worse. During her pre-Parkinson years, she was carefree. She would say what was on her mind without much of a filter. Luckily, she was also very kind-hearted so she rarely offended anyone. My mother's way of coping with difficult moments was to make light of the situation. My dad on the other hand took things way too seriously for most of his life. They truly were complete opposites in this regard. I remember when my mom first started to have tremors from Parkinson's, she nicknamed those episodes "ding-dong."

My dad did not find that funny at all. He had vivid childhood memories of an uncle also afflicted with Parkinson's disease who was always sad and depressed. My father could not understand my mom's sense of humor, especially during moments of tremors violent enough to shake his little car. He would get very annoyed with anyone who tried to make light of his wife's condition.

Many nights I saw my father drinking hard liquor before going to bed. I assumed that this was his way of coping with not only his wife's condition but also the shaking bed he shared with her.

Willingness to Change

Ruby & Jay

I wish I was more adept at debating, because convincing my seenagers to change required championship level debating skills.

Willingness to change was probably the most difficult topic for my parents and me. Dad did not mind change after he retired. Many a times he welcomed it, but that was generally after some careful planning on my part. I would start by planting seeds of change for weeks before bringing up the subject seriously. After a logical discussion, he would generally come to agree. My mom on the other hand was carefree for most of her life. But this changed when she started experiencing Parkinson's related tremors. From that point on, she began disliking change. Amazingly, had someone asked me during my childhood to rate my parents' level of comfort with change on a scale of one to ten, I probably would have rated my dad as being a two and my mom a nine. But that rating gradually flip-flopped as they aged.

From moving their bed one foot to the left to changing where they lived, were all tough discussions. Sometimes the smallest changes were most contentious. I never knew what reaction to expect. Change is hard at any age, but coupled with rapidly changing needs and changing personalities, it was much harder for mom and dad to absorb. This in turn only made it more difficult for me.

Who Defines "Well"?

Ruby

What the words "I am doing well today" meant was something different at every stage of their journey.

My mom did not want to experience any invasive procedures and she hated taking any medications. She would often say, "When it is time for me to go, accept it with grace and let me go, don't fight it." My mom and I did not see eye to eye on her health. Even when she would be shaking due to her Parkinson's disease, she would say, "I am doing very well." It was really difficult to convince her that if she would just let me take her to see her neurologist, he could adjust her medication to prevent the tremors.

After her death, I gave a charitable donation in my mom's name to the Michael J. Fox Foundation for Parkinson's Research. I learned a lot on their website that could have helped me be a better caregiver for her, but alas it was too late.

Advocating for Them

Ruby

Being well informed about the health condition is crucial to being a successful advocate. However, even when I thought I knew the best, it did not always turn out to be the right next step.

One day, I got a call from my dad in a panic, "Mom is not responding at all… They are calling an ambulance… What do I do?"

I responded to him in a calm voice, "I am here for you dad, let me talk to the nurse."

The nurse in the assisted living facility explained, "Your mom was at the dining table with her head down and your dad was trying to wake her up to eat for more than thirty minutes. We have tried everything and she shows no response. We had no choice but to call the ambulance. I think she has had a stroke."

I did not want to accept her analysis. "You know there are times that it is hard to wake her up from sleep," I told the nurse.

"I think this is different, she walked to the dining table, sat down and a minute later she was non-responsive," she argued.

I had to agree. The nurse put me on hold for a few minutes as the paramedics checked out my mom.

I could hear a number of distinct voices in the room but could not follow exactly what they were saying. The nurse came back on the phone after what seemed like hours, although it was probably just three minutes, and informed me, “They are taking her to the ER.”

My heart was pounding. “Will you be sending her to the Scripps Hospital?” I asked the nurse on the phone. “Please take care of dad, I know he will be very unsettled. Please let him know I will call him as soon as I start driving there.”

After several hours at the hospital it was confirmed that she did not have a stroke and it was “just a UTI – Urinary Tract Infection.” I have had few such infections over the course of my lifetime, but none that resulted in symptoms like hers. The “just a UTI” caused so much panic and grief for my over protective dad. I asked what we could do to prevent those in the future. The doctor in the ER said, “you can try to minimize those from happening by adding cranberry tablets daily to her diet and making sure that she keeps herself very clean. It’s not entirely possible to prevent these completely.” I knew that keeping her clean would not always be easy, given her Parkinson’s Disease.

Just a few weeks later she ended up in the ER again with the same symptoms. This time I had just come home from a difficult day at work with my boss. I had invited him over for dinner at my home as he was visiting from out of town. It was 7:30 pm and I was frantically trying to get dinner ready as my boss and husband socialized. I had not eaten all day. I was helping my ten-year-old daughter with her homework while I was cooking, when I got the call. "I am so sorry Rosie, but they are taking mom to the hospital again," said my tear-filled dad. I could barely hear him, as his voice was so low. I apologized to my boss, husband and daughter, dropped everything and drove to the ER.

A few hours later, my husband brought me some food on his way to drop my boss off to the airport. My daughter stayed up late that night even though she had a test the next morning. I stayed up all night waiting from my mom to wake up. At 4 am, she woke up and was fine. It was "just a UTI" again.

My mother had a couple of other UTI episodes when she moved in with my brother after my dad passed away. Luckily with the help of a great family doctor and the knowledge I now had from the two previous episodes, we were able to catch these before they became severe.

After a year at my brother's home my mom moved back to my home. Her health kept declining. One afternoon, she went to sleep for more than two days. No matter what we tried, we could not wake her. I thought that she probably had another UTI. I called her primary care physician and asked what we should do. "You should call the ambulance and take her to the ER," she told me. I followed the doctor's instructions and a day and a half later my mother was discharged when she finally woke up. This time, it was not a UTI. It was probably related to her Parkinson's disease which sometimes left her unresponsive for days.

Less than two weeks later, I learned that my mom had not passed urine in two days. Given that she was only drinking about one bottle of Glucerna (the nutritional shake) with not much else, I waited another twelve hours before calling her doctor. After her last ER visit, my mom had made it clear that she did not want to go back there under any circumstance.

"You need to take her to the ER," the doctor told me. I told mom I was instructed by her doctor to take her to the ER and I would get into trouble if I did not obey the doctor's instructions. Several hours into the ER visit, the doctor declared that she had another UTI. We were not sure if two weeks earlier the ER staff had not done proper testing or if this was newly acquired, but here we were once again.

“I am never coming to the ER again,” my mother told me in complete frustration.

After that episode, my mom continued to decline rapidly. I took her to her primary care physician and her neurologist for check-ups and to discuss her strong wish to not have to go to the ER again. Given her condition, they both agreed that she should be moved to palliative care (a.k.a hospice care or comfort care).

Focused Discussions

Mariya & Aliya

Steering the conversation in a focused direction was a challenge Lisa had to overcome.

Lisa's mom loved telling long stories and repeating them over and over again to her Aunt Mariya who suffered from Alzheimer's disease. Lisa would often tell her mom, "Yes mom, I have heard this already, but Aunt Mariya has not, so maybe you should tell her that story before she falls asleep." Aunt Mariya enjoying Lisa's mom's stories over and over again was a silver lining in the dark cloud of her Alzheimer's disease. It also gave Lisa a reprieve from having to listen repeatedly to the same stories. But Lisa's mom had a selective memory and she would only remember the things that suited her. She would frequently say things like, "You never told me that," even though Lisa and her dad both reminded her multiple times that they had. This was probably because she wanted to talk and would talk over whatever anyone else was saying. Lisa finally bought a smart phone for mom and taught her how to text.

She resorted to texting her mom for critical issues. These exchanges often went like this:

Lisa: “I met with an attorney today to discuss what dad wants to include in the will.”

Lisa’s mom: “So, what did the attorney say?”

Lisa: “I will call you at 6 pm tonight to discuss my conversation with the attorney.”

Another side benefit of texting was that Lisa’s mom would be ready and waiting to talk about the topic of the day that Lisa really needed to discuss with her without getting into her own long and repeated stories about her sister, her new-found friends or her day in general. She was also able to provide more thought out responses to the issues that Lisa had texted her about.

Isolation or Socialization

Aliya & Noah

Lisa wished that her mom and dad were not poles apart on the spectrum of socialization; from isolated to the extremely social.

Lisa's mom and dad were on opposite sides of the spectrum of isolation. Her dad did not want to go out of the house, and kept himself very isolated. Her mom on the other hand would attend all of the events at her church and Village, even when she was staying with her sister. Lisa's mom and dad fought constantly about her dad's isolation following retirement. Months would go by without him seeing anyone else but mom. The problem was that not only did he like to keep himself isolated, but he expected her mom to not socialize either. Being social was a huge part of her mom's life, and at her age she was not going to change.

Lisa knew that if she had to summarize in one word the reason for the end of her parents' marriage, it would be isolation. Her mom had moved in large part because she had wanted to help her aunt. However, a secondary reason had also been her feeling of being suffocated by her dad's constant criticism of her socialization.

Since she could not address her husband's isolation, she had made it her business to make sure no one else around her felt isolated.

Social Obligations

Aliya

Too much of a good thing like socialization proved to be a problem with Lisa's mom.

Lisa's mom made the purpose of her life to take care of other people's needs. She was always out and about meeting people and making new friends. Her normal day's agenda included meeting one to five people. She would always find a way to help others, if with nothing else with a friendly smile. Sometimes her friendships and her desire to help others came to the detriment of her own well-being.

Lisa remembers having many arguments with her mom like this one:

Lisa: "Mom, you don't sound good, can you please rest today."

Her mom: "No my dear, I promised Kate I would attend her baby shower, it won't look right if I don't go."

Lisa: "But mom, your body needs rest. Remember what you hear on planes, you have to put your own oxygen mask on first before helping others."

Her mom: “Honey, you know my view on the issue of rest all too well… Rest is what you do after you die.”

Even though, Lisa admired her mom’s caring personality and her love for people, she felt frustrated that she could not convince her mom to take better care of herself.

Family Grudges and Abandonment

Aliya & Noah

Lisa felt like she had super powers when she focused on tasks at hand rather than family grudges and abandonment.

Once Lisa's brother and his family came to visit her dad on their way to a vacation. He had told her that they were coming for Thanksgiving. As it turned out, they arrived at 8:00 pm on Wednesday night before Thanksgiving and left four hours later at midnight. Her dad had been waiting anxiously to see his son and family for months and looking forward to having Thanksgiving with them. Lisa had pre-cooked both a traditional Thanksgiving meal and a vegetarian meal for her sister-in-law. Her brother had told her, "We are getting there the night of Thanksgiving, and I am looking forward to being there."

Both Lisa and her dad had foolishly assumed that he would be spending the entire day with them. This really hurt him and for the first time Lisa heard her dad say, "I can't believe they just did that, that is just wrong. He should have let you know that they weren't staying for Thanksgiving." Knowing that her dad rarely verbalized his feelings and always kept his grudges well hidden from the world,

Lisa felt overwhelmed with sadness when she heard her dad speak those words.

The day Lisa's dad died, her mom was in different city with a broken ankle and needed help in getting to the funeral. Lisa's son was in the ER after suffering a concussion at a baseball game, her husband was out of the country for business and Lisa had the biggest deal of her career to negotiate. No one in Lisa's family stepped up to come and help her with the funeral. Lisa shared, "For a few days I got super powers that allowed me to accomplish all those things. Granted it was not to perfection, but somehow, I got everything done. If you ask me how I did it, I won't have an answer for you. It is all in a haze. I guess when you are in a tough situation with no choices and no one to help you, you just get things done."

Creative Compromises

Noah

Lisa had to get extremely creative in finding a compromise with a dad that was not willing to change.

Lisa claimed that by far she had not seen anyone else in her life that was more unwilling to change or compromise than her dad. She had lots of stories from her childhood about how her dad disliked change. He would get very upset even when she cut her hair a different style. Her mom had learned to ignore and laugh off his tirades when anything around him changed. Lisa felt that she was walking on egg shells with her dad when she wanted to change anything. This dynamic grew worse as he aged.

After Lisa's dad moved in with her, he expected her to do all his chores including picking up his clothes and shoes exactly the same way as her mom had. She neither had the time nor the energy for it. Even if she had magically found additional time to give to her dad, he would still complain to Lisa: "Your food does not taste like your mom's," or "You don't fold the clothes properly." These kinds of comments were ongoing irritants for Lisa.

Her dad who was accustomed to eating food freshly made first by his mom and then later by his wife. They had both catered to his wishes and had spoiled him. Her dad would often say to Lisa, "I would rather starve than eat yesterday's left-overs."

After months of dad's frequent hunger strikes when Lisa served left overs, she came up with a creative solution of freezing left overs and serving them the following week as fresh cooked meals. Given that her pleading to eat leftovers never worked, she thought a little lying was well worth the sin.

Lisa's dad was also extremely regimented about his daily routine. He wanted his meals promptly and wanted to leave home for appointments including parties on time. Lisa figured out that if she said, "we will leave sometime between 8:00 and 8:30 am," rather than "we will leave at 8:15 am," it minimized conflicts.

Humor Cure

Noah

Patience, playfulness and a good dose of humor can conquer the "I am not going to change" battle.

Lisa's husband had a wicked sense of humor that her dad fortunately enjoyed. Lisa would often enlist her husband's help when she and her dad got in a heated argument, mostly about her mom and their marriage. Even when her husband was out of town, Lisa would wait for him to come home to have a critical conversation with her dad.

If it were not for her husband's sense of humor, her parents' house would have remained unsold. Her dad would say, "I am not going to feel like a man if I sell my castle." Her husband would sit down with her dad and play a game of chess, and while dad was ahead in the game, he would take a break to get them whisky. Lisa would then join them and casually start talking about "dad's castle." Lisa's husband would talk about how dad's king and queen needed their castle. After a few months of discussing kings, queens and castles in a light-hearted manner, Lisa's dad acquiesced, "I guess it is time to let go of my castle and invest in my grandkid's castles."

He had insisted that he wanted to start an education savings account for his grandkids. He managed the money in their account, until he died.

Summary

One of the biggest sources of frustrations for both Lisa and I was having to deal with our extended families and siblings. We had no patience for family members sitting on the sidelines, passing judgment on our actions, giving unsolicited advice and above all feeding our seenagers with harmful recommendations.

Both Lisa and I had lots of stories about hanging up on our respective families, or not picking up their phone calls. The one thing that we laughed crazily about the first time we bonded was how our respective family members would say, "I am there for you." But there were no actions behind those words. Reflecting back on this, our hysterical laughter was our first big release of the hurt and abandonment we felt. We were both ready to release that huge burden we were carrying in laughter rather than in tears.

Some day we hope that we will be able to look back at the arguments and truly forgive and forget.

Chapter 4 – Exploring Home Options

Championing Change When Living at Home Becomes Unmanageable

Not wanting to move from a place where they had lived for a long time was natural for our seenagers. They could not admit their home was no longer suitable for them. The false narrative that their home was still a safe and comfortable place for them to live was their reality. We struggled with how to convince someone to change, if we couldn't help them face reality of their situation.

For some of them we had to repeatedly paint a picture of their home and their needs in a way they could understand and accept. The decision to move out of their home sometimes took years while other times, this change came overnight, as a result of a hospitalization.

We both learned quickly that no matter what living situation we were describing to them, we would always refer to it as, "your new home" or the "home better suited for your needs." Calling the living option as "my home," "assisted living," or "shared housing" only made them shut down.

Caregiving While in a City Far Away

Sami

Once I understood that money (not his health) would drive his decision to move, I used that to get the outcome that was best for us.

My uncle lived on the East Coast for a very long time. Over the years, many of his friends and family had moved away. He found himself getting more and more isolated and less able to live independently. I was able to find him caregivers online. I could also help him find resources for day-to-day chores like grocery shopping, driving, gardening and more. I could get the resources to show up at his doorstep, but could not make him like them or accept the help. Unfortunately, he almost always had a reason why the resources I found were not good enough. His top reasons were: too expensive, not trustworthy, not punctual or just incompetent. He also came up with other unique reasons from time to time: "She wears too much perfume," or "I just don't like the way he laughs."

Uncle Sami used to take lots of painkillers and constantly complain. "My lower back, hips and knees are really hurting today." When I would try to make suggestions like, "Can we please make an appointment with your doctor?" or "Can we get you a massage chair?" or "Can I find you a trainer to help you stretch?" The answer was always a firm "No."

Finally, my uncle ended up in the ER because of a fall down the stairs. I must have heard him narrate the same story a million times over. "I woke up in the morning with very bad back pain. I had left my painkillers downstairs so I had to go down for them. As I was taking the last step, I tried to hurry, and I fell…"

When he ended up in the ER and was complaining about his pain, they decided to run a few tests and keep him overnight in the hospital. The hospital's decision sounded unusual. I happened to be just a short drive away from his home on a business trip, so I drove to the hospital to see him. It was then that they diagnosed him with prostate cancer.

As he went through surgery, chemotherapy and radiation, I could not always be there for him physically or even respond to his needs in a timely manner. I found it increasingly difficult to put my life on hold and to fly out there for each short acute or chronic health crisis at hand. However, I was unable to convince him to move to San Diego to be near me, so I could be a better advocate for him.

One day while he was in the hospital, he had a conversation with nurse about property values in California. She had just relocated from California and was able to buy a mansion. He asked me that day "So how much have home prices appreciated over the last ten years?" When I shared with him that the price of my home had doubled, he seemed shocked and said, "I can't believe that. The price of my home is the same as the day I bought it eons ago."

The next time I visited him, I came prepared with stats to show him, the major difference in property appreciation in San Diego compared to where he lived. Since the majority of his decisions were based on finances, I could not believe I had not tried that angle with him earlier.

Needless to say, we started the process of looking for a house and he moved to San Diego within eight months.

Shared Housing a Win-Win Situation

Sami

My uncle considered my Win-Win solution to his predicament flawed.

When my uncle moved to San Diego he bought a two-story house. “This will be a better investment, it will appreciate more,” he said.

“What are you going to do with the second floor?” I asked him, knowing that he had bad knees and could not climb up the steps. He just shrugged in response.

I knew one of my widowed neighbors, Jane, had found a new roommate. It had really changed her life. She seemed a lot happier after the roommate moved in. They were doing a lot of fun stuff together. Jane had told me that her new roommate had introduced her to San Diego Oasis and they had been enjoying taking exercise and dancing classes there.

One day, I ran into Jane and her roommate in a coffee shop and I asked them, “Have you guys had a fight yet?” They looked at each other warmly and responded, “Only about the Keystone pipeline.” They each described their views to me with intense passion.

“Things seem to be working out really well for you. How did you guys find each other?” I asked them. They told me how they had both registered with Elder Help of San Diego. They told me all about this non-profit that did not charge either of them for this matching service. Jane provided more details, acting as if she was a spokesperson for Elder Help. “This organization vets both homeowners and seniors looking for housing. They also find out details about what you are looking for in a housemate, such as likes and dislikes. Once Elder Help identified that we could be a good match, they had us meet and we had an instant connection.”

The same day I told my uncle about Elder Help of San Diego and insisted that he go on their website to see if he would be interested in participating.

“I am not sure about this now, but maybe when I am older and can’t live by myself. It would be better than moving to an old folk’s home,” he said to me the next day. I had come ready to bargain with him that day. I was feeling a tremendous pressure with me having become his only social interaction now that he had moved to San Diego.

I said “Okay, if you won’t consider that, I have an alternate suggestion I know you will really enjoy. I really want you to listen to what I have to say with an open mind.” He nodded, I took that nod as that is the best I am going to get out of him today and said, "How about Improv?" His eyes lit up, "Did you get us tickets to go see improv?"

I added, "No I did one better, I have signed you up for this class called 'Introduction to Improv'." Sensing his disappointment that it was not an evening out to watch improv, I quickly started to line up all the reasons why he should join the class. "You know I have already paid a non-refundable fee." Money matters were always good reasons for him to take action, so I started with that. "It's at San Diego Oasis, I have heard a lot of great things about that organization. Can you go for at least three classes and if you don't like it, I won't force you to go?" I said that knowing full well that he would go to all the classes that I had already paid for, because he would be the last one to leave any money on the table.

Turned out he not only enjoyed the improv classed I had signed him up for, he decided to sign-up for it again and again.

Even though I felt he should not be living alone, it was a battle I did not win with him until the last few months of his life when he was on complete bed rest.

We found someone amazing to move in to the second story of his home. This person took over all the chores around the house in return for free place to stay. It was a win-win situation.

Caregiving from Another Country

Ruby & Jay

In hindsight, I feel I worried more when my parents were in another country. The feeling of helplessness drove me crazy when they had an issue that could not be easily resolved.

When I first took on the caregiving role for my parents they lived in another country. I was not there for their day-to-day needs, and could not physically get things done for them. I didn't have a network of family, friends, neighbors or providers I could rely on. Getting there in a timely manner was impossible, even when they were diagnosed with a critical need following an operation. I had a real tough time putting my life on hold and flying out at a short notice for each acute or chronic health crisis, let alone a smaller crisis like, "Our fridge is not working and we need a new one." I would find myself helplessly saying, "How can I help you?" knowing full well that there was no good answer coming back from them.

One time my mom called me on a Monday evening at 5:00 pm. I had never heard her as scared as she sounded that day. "Your father just had a heart attack and was taken to the hospital. He is going into a triple bypass surgery soon."

I could clearly sense that she wanted and needed me there by her side. Unfortunately, I had just put my passport in the mail for renewal previous Friday. To top that off, I had slipped while on a steep hike the previous weekend and my right hand was in a splint. I did not know how I was going to pull it off, but I felt I had no choice but to get their as fast as I could. I was able to get a temporary passport and was on a plane in less than thirty hours after the call.

I guess on one level, I could have chosen to be an ostrich with my head in the sand, and not think about my parents, or not call them and go on about my life. Of course, this was something I was not capable of doing. Occasionally, I did not talk to them on the phone for days and I would successfully become an ostrich during those brief moments. But inevitably, things would happen around me reminding me of them and at night the guilt monster would attack me and convert me from an ostrich to a daughter again.

When They Were Living with Me

Ruby & Jay

I worried less when they were living with me, but I was intimately involved in their day to day needs. I was helping them take one day at a time and make the most of it.

I faced my parents' ups and downs as I checked in on them in the morning before I left home and again in the evening. They would take on my mood and I theirs. In the mornings I would always ask, "How was your night?" and in the evening, "How was your day?" Sometimes, I would get really long answers as they wanted to engage me in conversation and get me to interact with them for as long as they could. I found myself getting irritated with them for giving me such long answers and making me late for work.

In time, I figured out how to have a pleasant discussion with them every morning by saying, "I hope you had a great night and pray that you will have a wonderful day." What I was trying to do was acknowledge the previous night in a positive tone, set a path forward for the upcoming day, and also give them a little project to keep them busy.

I would say things to them like, “I really need for you to say a special prayer for me,” or “Can you say a prayer for your granddaughter, she has a difficult test today.” I would also add things like, “It is going to be an exceptionally beautiful day today, can you please go for a walk around the neighborhood and stop by the neighbor’s home and ask them for the gardener’s phone number?” or “your grandson needs to learn chess for his Boy Scouts merit badge, can you please teach him how to play when he gets home from school?” By giving them with a couple of options of things to do, I wanted them to feel they were in charge of the day.

I found that giving them a project to do during the day helped them to feel productive. At night, I would ask for a status on their project or provide status on how well their prayers worked. I would end the conversation by saying, “I think we all need a good night’s sleep after a productive day today.” This would usually make them feel that they accomplished something and their life had meaning. And in fact, it truly did.

Since I was not spending time just getting to where they lived, I was able to spend more quality time with them dealing with their emotional issues. I was eventually able to get to a point where I could have short succinct conversations with them, as they knew that the next conversation was not that far away.

Could Not Avoid Skilled Nursing Facility

Eli

Skilled Nursing Facility (SNF – Pronounced Sniff) is generally paid for by the insurance, but you normally have a choice on which one your loved one is transferred to from a hospital.

One day, I heard my mom screaming while I was cooking dinner. I ran to her and found that my dad had fallen on the bathroom floor. Turned out that he had suffered a heart attack. He was hospitalized for several days. When he was being discharged from the hospital the doctor told me, "We will discharge him to a SNF." I asked, "What is a sniff?". He replied kindly, "Its SNF – Skilled Nursing Facility, these facilities provide rehab care to Medicare/Medicaid patients. This is a bridge between hospital care and home." I was given a list of insurance-approved facilities within a twenty-mile radius of where we lived.

I toured a few and since it was my first time going through this experience, I approved one that was not too far but looked the cleanest and had the friendliest staff. If I had to do this over again, I would look at other criteria such as: the physicians affiliated with the facility, frequency of physician visits, overall facility rating and patient satisfaction. I would also sneak a chance to talk to a primary caregiver hanging around a patient, and ask about the physical and occupational therapy regimen, and insist on meeting with the social worker that would be assigned to work with my dad.

My dad's insurance paid for the service, but the level of care and number of days he was able to stay there was something I fought hard to influence for my dad's benefit.

Choosing an Option with Short Notice

Ruby & Jay

It was tough finding a perfect option for a place for my parents to live with a short notice, limited budget and health challenges.

When my dad was discharged from the hospital into a Skilled Nursing Facility (SNF), I felt paralyzed with panic. He had been the primary caregiver for my mom. How would I be able to take care for both of them at home when he was discharged from the SNF?

My parents' bedroom was located on the ground level, and was not big enough to accommodate the constant use of an oxygen tank. Besides that, my father did not have enough strength to help my mom in and out of bed anymore. How would I possibly help them manage their medications? These feelings of powerlessness and frustration seemed insurmountable. What was I going to do?

Even if I got my home miraculously transformed to accommodate my parents' new needs, I would need help in providing round-the-clock care for them. I called a friend of mine that owned an in-home service provider agency. Even with friendship discounts it was going to cost me about $20/hour. I needed round the clock care for them. So, the quick math of 365 days a year, twenty-four hours a day, at $20/hour added up to a whopping $175,000/year. This was not a viable option.

The second day my dad was in the SNF, I talked with a social worker there. I described my predicament and she assured me that my situation with my parents was not the most difficult one she had ever encountered. She introduced me to Jan, who specialized in finding support and housing for people like us.

Assisted living or room and board were the two options that Jan presented to us. She gave me a list of three of each and asked me to go visit them. These were possible options that fell within our budget, but none of which were comfortable enough that I would consider living there myself.

The room and board options were houses with about six residents in each. The first one had a very small bedroom where maneuvering the wheelchair and oxygen tank would have been difficult. The next one seemed to have a very sad atmosphere with four of the residents in wheelchairs sleeping in front of a TV with a smell of urine in the air. This was not something that I could let my parents experience. The last place was owned by someone who seemed like a harsh warden rather than a gentle caregiver. All of these residences had either Caucasian or African American residents and given the differences in culture, language, and food, I could not imagine my mom and dad very comfortable there.

Later, I visited the three assisted living places. The owner of the first one was from the same ethnic background as our family, but the room was the most expensive of them all, and way outside of what we could afford. The next one was much too far away from my home and work, making it very difficult for me to visit even once a week. The final one was within budget, 20 miles from where I lived and had a big comfortable room that was clean and basic. Even though I did not feel comfortable with the dining hall, shared spaces and some of the other residents, I felt this was the best of the worst choices.

Assisted Living and the PACE Program

Ruby & Jay

Given all the limitations, the combination of assisted living with the PACE program was truly the best option for my parents.

The assisted living facility I finally chose for my parents provided all the daily services my parents needed in an apartment style environment. Everything from housekeeping, nursing, dining, wellness activities, limited transportation, bathing assistance, personal care and medication management.

I felt horrible about moving my parents into that assisted living facility and prayed real hard that God would give us the strength to accept the situation and see the place they were living in with loving eyes. My dad made friends with the caregivers, med-tech, nurse, chef, cleaning crew and executive director. My mom on the other hand would say, “It is very depressing to be around so many old people.” She started to sleepwalk while in that facility and would try to escape in the middle of the night. Sometimes they had to really strong-arm her to take her back to their bedroom. All of her life she had been a kind, soft-spoken person who would not hurt a fly, but during these sleepwalking episodes, she would get really angry and occasionally become physically violent with anyone who tried to stop her in her tracks. I felt so helpless hearing about her episodes.

I would visit them several times a week and initially I would take them out for a drive to the beach. However, as time passed their conditions worsened and neither one wanted to leave their bedroom.

In this assisted living facility, they highly recommended that the residents not keep any valuables, including cash or credit cards. They did not want to take a chance with theft from staff members. My parents were able to keep some money with the assisted living facility just like a bank deposit. This was one of the hardest things for my dad. To this day, I wish I had just kept a $20 bill in his jacket to make him feel more in control. I can't forget the disappointment and horror on his face when I took his wallet from him and told him he could not keep it with him. I think that day part of his pride died and his health began to decline rapidly.

My father did not bring up the desire to keep his wallet with him after that day. However, he hardly went out of the assisted living to buy anything. I encouraged him many times to go for a walk outside and get some candy from the grocery store. He probably did that six times in the year that he lived there.

I was there for most of the physical needs that my parents had: including going with them to the hospital on one hand, or buying dad toothpicks he desperately needed on the other hand. I had a hard time carving out time to be there for them emotionally. Taking the time to sit down calmly and patiently to address their emotional needs was difficult.

It is hard for me to admit this but part of the reason I had a hard time was because I did not like the assisted living facility that they were in. I was the one who had found it and had convinced them to move there. It was the best we could afford. It made me sick to go to the assisted living facility because I could not stand the smell or the sad looks on some of the residents' faces.

My mom used to tell me that she was unhappy "because the people here are too old." When I would respond to my mom by saying, "But mom, there are many residents here that are younger than you," she would point to someone sitting on a bench. Even if that person was smiling at us, my mom would say, "you are wrong, look she is so sad." I now think it was a reflection of how she truly felt.

The best thing that the assisted living place introduced me to was St. Paul's PACE (Program of All-inclusive Care for the Elderly), a program fully covered by California's Medi-Cal (Medicaid elsewhere in the country). This program was a God send. St. Paul's PACE facility was located a few miles away from my parent's assisted living and had a primary care doctor, nurses, nutritionist, lab, dentist, occupational and physical therapist, plus counseling. The great thing about the PACE program was they actually worked together on each patient as a team and provided transportation to their facility. They also coordinated directly with the assisted living facility to make sure my parents were ready for their appointments.

Even with that huge level of support, the practical things I needed to do for them, along with my own responsibilities, left no time for me to tackle my own health issues, exercise and let alone have time for recreation. I found myself not being able to do everything as well as I liked. My relationship with my spouse suffered in spite of having a strong foundation.

I visited them four to six times a week and checked in with them, their doctor or the director of assisted living on a daily basis.

Active Retirement Community

Ruby, Jay, Sami

If I could not live at home as I age, I would want to be in an Active Retirement Community.

Leisure or active lifestyle oriented communities (LORCS) include various amenities. A retirement community is a housing complex designed for seenagers who are generally able to care for themselves. However, assistance from home care agencies is allowed in some communities, and activities and socialization opportunities are often provided. Many high-end LORCS even have a private golf course exclusively for the residents. One such facility called Brookdale exists less than three miles from where I live. I had hoped that one day I would have enough money to move my parents there, but it was well out of our price range.

My uncle could have certainly afforded to live in one of these communities for many more years than he lived, but he had a hard time parting with his money and I could not convince him to even go tour one of them with me. His sense of isolation would have certainly been addressed by living there. He would have people to eat meals with, go out and play golf with, keep his place clean, do his laundry and much more. And as he declined he could have received more services such as medication management, which is something he progressively got worse at over the years.

Memory Care Facilities

Mariya

Lisa's mom was so against what she called "institutional facilities" that the family did not consider moving her aunt into memory care facilities.

Memory care facilities would have provided her aunt with all the daily services she would need in an apartment or condo style environment. It would have even included housekeeping, nursing care, dining services, wellness activities, limited transportation, personal care and medication management. Plus, the added lock-down, security and much higher level of oversight would have kept her aunt safe from family and caregiver abuse.

This rational reasoning did not work with Lisa's mom, plus her cousin would probably not have wanted the extra expense of such a facility. Lisa did not feel it was her place to push the issue, even though she felt that this was the best solution for Aunty Mariya once her Alzheimers got worse.

Room and Board

Aliya & Mariya

It was very hard for Lisa to find a three-way match between her aunt, her mom, and any room and board facilities she was able to evaluate.

Lisa also explored room-and-board accommodations, which take care of six to ten residents in a house-like setting. When Lisa found out that these types of facilities are family owned and operated with no oversight or regulations enforcing sensible standards, this put a real doubt in her mind.

She still investigated a few places when they were struggling with the family interactions between Lisa's mom and her aunt's kids, whose home they were living in. However, she found that it was hard to match her mom and aunt's personalities with the caregivers of the facilities she explored. Her mom was willing to move into one even though she really didn't need the type of care they provided, just so that she would be with her sister.

Given the intimate setting of these houses, it was important to see how her mom and aunt would fit-in with the other residents. In the end, Lisa gave up this idea as she did not find one that had the right combination of location, facility, cost, services, care takers and residents that would meet both her mom and aunt's needs and personalities.

Aging in the "Village"

Aliya

Lisa fell in love with the concept of Villages when she saw the impact of it on her mom's life. Her mom was less isolated, more independent, filled with purpose and overall healthier.

When Lisa's mom moved in with her aunt in Kansas City, Lisa was looking for ways to keep her mom busy, and not have her focus solely on her aunt. She knew that her mom would need social connections. She recalled watching the NBC news segment done by Brian Williams about the "Village Movement," where neighbors help each other age in place. She recalled that some villages have an active social calendar and encourage volunteerism and other activities that her mom would enjoy. Lisa did a search and found the Village to Village Network website with a map of all the Villages in the country. She was able to find a "Village" close to where Aunt Mariya lived. The social calendar seemed amazing with classes of all kinds within walking distance from her mom. The calendar included things like; social gatherings for all major holidays, fun outings, yoga classes, healthy eating group, singing club, etc.

This Village also had a bartering system allowing its members to exchange favors with each other, using favor points. Since Lisa's mom was a wonderful cook, she often cooked meals for others, and in return she would save up favor points that her sister would be able to redeem for favors and companionship when she was not with her. The village even had a care team that would get involved in the event Lisa's aunt would end up in the hospital or just needed someone to help her count her medicine or see what refills she needed to order and when. Lisa and her mom both thought they had hit a jackpot when Lisa found this village concept so near to her aunt's home.

Unfortunately, when Lisa's mom tried to enroll her sister in the "aging-in-place village," the executive director came to her home to talk to her sister and insisted that she needed to talk with her kids. The Executive Director said this was necessary because they were involved in deciding care solutions for her aunt. After talking to Lisa's aunt's daughter-in-law, the Executive Director decided not to accept Lisa's aunt as a member because she claimed that she was "too dependent on others to qualify for our program." Lisa's mom suspected that the true reason for refusing Lisa's aunt's admission into the village was that she saw a dysfunctional family dynamic between her aunt and her daughter-in-law and did not want the other village members to get thrown in the fray of the arguments. Her mom's suspicion seemed accurate when the Executive Director told

Lisa, "your aunt can be a temporary member while your mom is a member of the village and living with her."

While Lisa's mom was part of the village, both her mom and her aunt became very socially active. Her mom used to say: "Our village people have reminded my sister how to laugh and live again."

Lisa's mom became very independent because of the village. Lisa was delighted to hear from her mom: "Our sink was leaking and I used one of my favor points to have someone come and fix it for us. I didn't even tell your cousin that we had a problem. I just got it fixed, with MY favor points."

It was clear to Lisa that her mom had gained confidence by being a part of the village and was feeling more independent. This was a stark difference from the panicked call she had received from her mom one day when her dad was not feeling well and the toilet was clogged. Lisa recalled how hard it had been to find the right plumber on the Internet and arrange for him to go to her parents' home for an emergency visit to unclog the toilet.

Living Alone at Home

Noah

Lisa's dad had to be convinced that his home was no longer his safe haven.

When Lisa's mom moved in with her aunt, her dad was adamant that he would live in the house by himself. Since her dad did not like to cook, Lisa had to figure out a solution for meals. After trying many options, she finally found a nutritionist willing to come to her dad's home and cook for him five days a week. Lisa had a freshly made meal delivery company deliver the meals for the other two days. Knowing that her dad expected freshly cooked meals daily, this was a must solve problem.

In the three years that Lisa's dad lived alone, she felt like she tried everything under the sun to try and convince him to move. She brought him to her home for a vacation; she went and visited him by herself; she had her husband visit him for a "man-to-man" conversation; she had her kids write letters; she had her doctor tell him; she took him to visit active retirement communities. None of that worked. He was stubborn and set in his ways. She kept trying different things because each time he would say, "Let me think about it," and follow that up with a lot of questions. His analysis paralysis on this subject drove Lisa nuts.

In the meantime, his big house was getting run down both inside and out since he was not able to care of it. If Lisa would send someone to take care of the garden or clean the house he would fire them and then tell Lisa, "They just weren't doing it right, even after I told them how I wanted it."

After he was diagnosed with fibromyalgia and he was on heavy painkillers, he got very depressed. One day he overdosed on the medication. Lisa kept calling him all evening and when he did not answer, she finally called a neighbor to go knock on his door. When he still did not answer, they called the police to come and break in. They found him non-responsive in bed. He was taken to the ER and hospitalized for a few days. They were trying to determine if that was an attempt at suicide or if he had genuinely forgotten. He convinced everyone that it was just a mistake.

While he was in the hospital Lisa told him, "Dad I am not asking you this time, I am telling you that you are moving in with us. I have started packing up already and have booked your tickets. You are coming and staying with us. It is a one-way ticket and we will figure out what is best for you once you have fully recovered."

Summary

As caregivers, we were never satisfied fully with the living arrangement, nor were our seenagers. The options we did not select always looked better in hindsight.

The reality of not being able to live independently is a tough pill to swallow for anyone, let alone for someone who is set in their own ways.

Both Lisa and I faced the difficult challenge of needing round-the-clock care for our loved ones and the hardship of how much it would cost, even at minimum wage. If we found someone on craigslist.com at $10/hour for twenty-four hours a day and 365 days a year, it would cost about $90,000 per year. That also meant taking on the risk of vetting them ourselves, and finding someone stable that was going to stick around for as long as we needed them. On the other hand, when I called my friend who owns an agency that deploys vetted, trained, licensed and insured resources to do this job, the cost was going to be double that amount, even with a deep friend's discount she was willing to offer me.

I guess there are no great solutions. We picked the ones that we thought were best at the time and lived with the consequences.

Chapter 5 – Keeping Them Safe & Secure

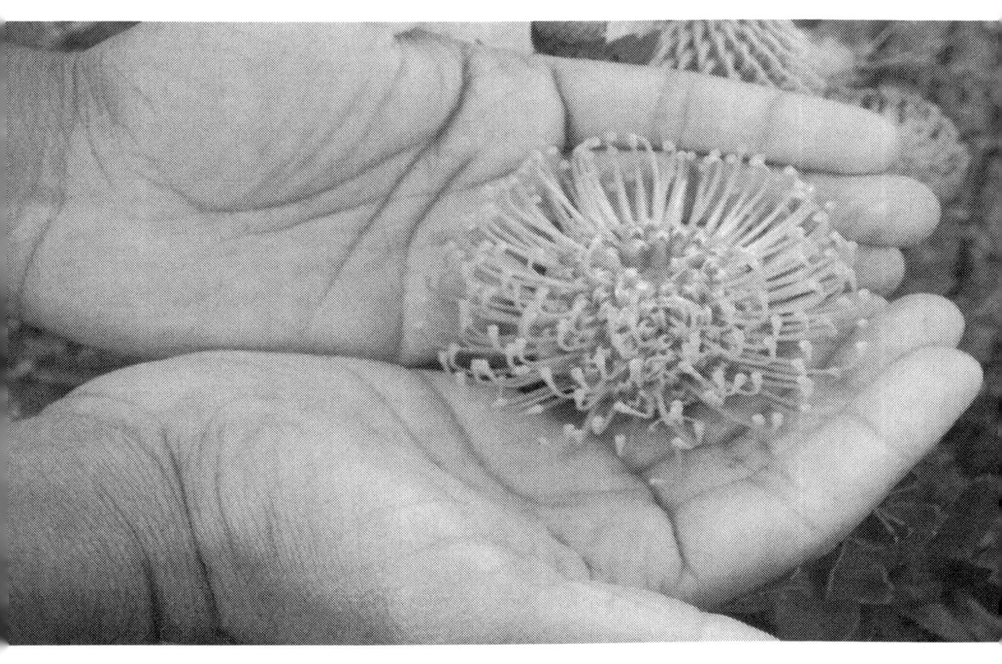

Life Is Fragile

There were so many unique daily living, safety and security concerns that both Lisa and I had to overcome. One metric for determining how well my seenagers were doing was keeping track of their eating habits. The other was bringing up a semi-controversial topic to see if they would react normally, be irritated or have no reaction.

The common thread with these stories is that every time they reached a new low, both Lisa and I had to get involved with our respective seenagers to help them emotionally and/or physically adjust to the "new norm." Besides finding a new solution or a new guardrail, effective situational communication was the essential ingredient to effective caregiving.

Treasure Hunting for Finances

Sami & Ruby

Keeping them safe sometimes required funds, so it was important to figure out any hidden places that they may have savings.

Long-Term Care

One month before my uncle passed he told me that he had a long-term care insurance policy that he had taken out on himself when he was fifty. He used to say, "I have made sure I am taken care of in my old age." I did not know until then that he was referring to this long-term care insurance policy. Realizing that he had had this available all along frustrated me to the point of wanting to scream out loud. Even less than two years prior to this point when I would ask him if I could arrange for some help for him he would say, "I don't want to spend my money on that." It took me six months after his death to recover the money for his expenses in the last months that he was alive. Neither Lisa nor my other seenagers had long-term care insurance.

Jewelry Artwork Collectibles

My uncle had a hobby of collecting model and miniature airplanes. He had one room in his home with a big table in the middle of the room with painted runways dedicated to the display of those planes. My uncle spent hours in that room every day without telling us what he did there, but we all knew this was more than a hobby or pass time. When he died, we had a collector evaluate and buy his collection. It was worth over $127,000.

Business ownership

My uncle had made investments in several startup companies. He had a folder for each company, and when I started managing his finances I had to go through each of the ten companies that he had invested in anywhere from $5,000 to $10,000 to see if that ownership could be liquidated. One of those companies had shares that had grown one hundred times from the original amount. It took a lot of time and administrative paperwork to get everything divested. However, it was well worth doing as the total dollar amount after all the sales was over $250,000.

Social Security Disability Income

By the end of my mom's life when we were running out of the savings we had set aside for her, I realized that she would be eligible for SSDI (Social Security Disability Income). It seemed like a long and laborious process to get approval, but I said to myself, "No pain, no gain" and started the process. It would not have been enough by any means to cover for her expenses, but it could have helped. Unfortunately, she passed away before SSDI was approved for her.

Preventing Over Eating

Sami

I employed begging for forgiveness rather than asking for permission in coming up with creative ways to control my uncle's bad eating habits.

My uncle had a bad habit of overeating and would eat a lot of junk food. Especially when he was in his "official room—the room where he kept all his model airplanes, as well as a fridge and a small pantry stocked with harmful foods. When I would visit him, I would sneak into his room and replace some of those items with healthy snacks. I would always get a phone call less than an hour after my visit from him, telling me how upset he was that I had gone in his "official room" and "mucked up his stuff". He would follow up with a thank you for the snacks I had replaced (if he liked them). I am sure he threw away the ones he did not like.

It was easier to just do stuff for my uncle than to ask him for his permission. Later, whenever he got upset about my intervention into his day-to-day life decisions, I would simply apologize profusely. "I am so, so sorry, I should not have assumed you would like for me to hire the exterminator for your kitchen. I had seen so many ants that I thought it would be useful. Please forgive me."

I learned over time to avoid saying things like, "but I thought that would be better for you." This statement was a trigger which only earned me responses from him like, "How many times have I told you that what you think is better for me is not necessarily good for me." Begging for forgiveness rather than asking for permission was something that I really got good at eventually.

Identity Theft

Sami

Getting legal help was necessary to rectify the identity theft my uncle experienced.

When my uncle handed over the keys to his kingdom to me, along with a number of unpaid credit card bills, I found some very unusual charges on his credit card statements. These were for things that I knew my uncle would never purchase. These charges were all on two credit cards, which my uncle assured me he did not have. It eventually turned out that his identity had been stolen and someone else had applied for and received credit cards in his name and were making purchases.

I tried to resolve this for several months on my own and then I called 211 for help. They recommended "Legal Aid Society of San Diego." They explained the complexity of the situation and suggested I hire an attorney. I agreed with them. I just wish I had thought of doing so earlier.

Online Theft

Sami

Having good long passwords (at least 12 characters) would have prevented online theft.

My uncle who thought he was very tech savvy and used the Internet for many of his tasks did not understand the concept of cyber security, and refused to listen to reason. One day his iPhone was stolen while he was at a neighborhood bar.

As it turns out, the culprit was a teenager who stole his iPhone, as a form of revenge when my uncle got him kicked out of a bar for being underage. "You cannot serve alcohol to that brat," my uncle had said while pointing his finger at the geeky kid. The teen understood from my uncle's action that he was about to be thrown out of the bar and on his way out picked up my uncle's iPhone that he had left on the table.

Unfortunately, my repeated pleading to have him change his password for his phone to anything other than 1234 had reached deaf ear. The geeky kid was not only able to get into his phone, but he was able to find a file called "keys to my kingdom" which contained all of my uncle's passwords. The kid then went on Amazon and ordered six iPhones and had them delivered to my uncle's address. Since he knew where my uncle lived and when the iPhones were going to arrive, he went and picked them up from the porch. To be malicious, the kid either changed passwords to many of his other accounts or just deleted them.

To top it off, my uncle did not tell me about any of this until the next day, when I showed up at his doorstep because he was not answering his phone. We could have traced the phone and wiped the data, had he told us right away. The police were eventually able to catch the teenager my uncle had proudly identified by telling them, "I know who should be your Prime Suspect."

"I want to make sure we can find your phone right away, if this were to happen again. Can you let me have your AppleID and Password?" I took the opportunity to convince my uncle. The biggest silver lining of all was that I was now able to access his iPhone and monitor where he was in case he was not answering my calls.

When He Was Paranoid

Eli

I felt helpless to see my kind dad become so paranoid of others.

One time when my dad was in the hospital with a bad case of COPD, they suspected that he may also have tuberculosis, so they moved him into an "isolation unit." Gown, gloves, and masks were required for anyone that entered his room. I saw the most change in his personality at that time and it really threw me off. He started to suspect that the people around him were out to get him. He thought that they were keeping him there for malicious reasons and that they were changing the temperature of the room to keep him uncomfortable. Also, he constantly declared that no one came to help him in spite of him ringing the bell over and over again. There was not much I could say or do to convince him that the reality he was describing in fact did not exist, but it was gut wrenching to see him so in such emotional torment.

The day after he was finally moved out of isolation into a shared room in the hospital, he pointed at the patient across the room and said, "That man keeps staring at me. I am not sure what he wants to take from me. I think you should take home all my belongings and even my wedding band. He was looking at that earlier." He acted so out of character, that it felt someone had taken over the soul in his body.

I left the room and could not hold my tears. The other man's son was standing there and reached out to me, "Are you okay?"

"Was your dad staring at mine earlier today?" I asked him.

"No, he has been in a coma all day."

I slipped down to the floor, put my head down and took some deep breaths. I knew I needed to compose myself and go back in to address his other concerns.

My dad then told me, "I keep ringing the bell for help, but I think the doctor does not like me and he must have told all the nurses not to respond to me. No one comes when I ring the bell for help."

"Dad, I am going to get that fixed for you. Do you believe me?" I told him in the most loving calm voice and a smile on my face. I think he was getting sleepy again, with his eyelids dropping and he responded, "I believe you." He smiled back at me and went to sleep. I knew that arguing with him about his paranoid claims was going to be detrimental for both of us. Instead, I entered into his reality and assured him that I was going to take care of things for him –

which made him feel heard. In the end, this was all that he needed at that time. On one hand, it made me feel like I was being sneaky by going into a world that my dad had created, but on the other hand, I knew that was the only place I could meet him and have a peaceful and loving conversation.

Loss of Hearing

Eli

I struggled with convincing my dad that his loss of hearing was making him unsafe.

My dad was hard of hearing but remained in denial about his hearing up until the very end. I always found this surprising because he would usually listen to most suggestions made by his doctor or me but obtaining a hearing aid was an exception. Even after a couple of hearing tests that proved he had a hearing loss problem, my dad grudgingly agreed to the purchase of hearing aids, but rarely wore them. It was an issue for his safety when he went walking on the street and could not hear a car or biker coming behind him.

To this day, it stays a mystery why he did not want to admit he had a hearing problem. Even though we did not have an incident we all would have regretted, it caused me undue worry.

Medicine Management

Jay & Ruby

Medication management for my mom was a real challenge because she did not want to take them.

I often struggled with medication management for my parents. Even though my father had pillboxes that helped him stay organized, he had his own system. I could never figure out how he kept organized given the seventeen pills, two nasal sprays and two inhalers he and my mom needed to take daily. When my parents moved into assisted living this responsibility became the duty of med techs. My dad changed his role to quality control. When the med tech would hand over the meds my mom needed to take, my dad would first check to see if everything was right, before nodding at mom to take the meds. My dad would make a fuss anytime a new batch of meds were either a different color or size.

After my dad passed and I hired caregivers to be with my mom twenty-four hours a day, she would often refuse to take her meds.

"I have done meds for too long, and I don't want them anymore," she would say. I would intervene and tell her, "but mom, you will shake."

“I don’t care,” she would say. We would argue several times a week, and sometimes I had to just give up. Other times, if the meds were critical, I added them to apple sauce, her nutritional shake or any other food that could possibly hide them.

Home Hazards Fall Prevention

Ruby

I knew all too well about baby proofing my home, because I had a very active and curious son. I had never thought I would have to seenager proof my home.

When my mom started falling, I got very paranoid about her every move. I was able to find that Jewish Family Services had a "Fix-It Service" program. At no charge to us they sent a trained volunteer to our home to analyze our situation and make recommendations to make our home safer for mom.

He recommended installing grab bars, moving carpets, putting in extra lighting and more. During that visit, he was able to install grab bars near the toilet and shower. He also installed guard rails on my mom's bed. With his expert eyes looking at my mom's surroundings and movement throughout the house, I am sure we prevented many falls.

Losing Sight

Ruby

As my mom started losing her sight, it not only affected her physical movements around the house, but also her favorite pastime, which was reading. Her new pastime became sleeping.

My mom was an avid reader. When she started to lose her sight, it became increasingly difficult to keep her busy and safe. Pretty soon, my mom began substituting sleep for all her activities, and would sleep about twenty hours a day. This shift was a key reason for her decline. We tried cataract surgery, eye exams, magnifying glasses, but nothing really worked for her.

My daughter would occasionally play songs from old movies and her favorite artists on YouTube for her grandmother. One day my daughter asked me, "Can we get an iPad for grandma for Mother's Day? I will teach her how to use YouTube. She really enjoys when I play something for her on my iPad from YouTube."

Given that she was not able to dial on her cell phone properly. I was not very hopeful that she would learn how to search and play movies and TV shows on YouTube. However, since my daughter was so insistent, I thought it was worth trying, besides I did not have time to look for another gift for Mother's Day. My daughter did a great job, and it really turned out to be the best gift for my mom at that stage of her life. It also gave a reason for my daughter and mom to spend more time together. I noticed that on the days that she was busy on her iPad she would stay awake for longer periods of time and eat properly. I am so grateful to my daughter for finding a solution where I was beginning to think none existed.

Personal Hygiene

Ruby

Helping her keep up with personal hygiene sometimes required more patience than with a child.

When my mom was experiencing dementia episodes she would at times forget how to turn on the tap, or would try to use the toothpaste tube as a toothbrush.

She had to be gently reminded with words like, "Oh, this is the cleaning side of the tooth brush that goes in your mouth, right mom?" Wording it as a question for which she knew the answer worked a whole lot better than saying, "Mom you are using the toothpaste tube as a tooth brush." Depending on her mood she would either respond back by saying, "No, I AM NOT," or just give me a really puzzled look.

Poor Judgment of Capability

Ruby

I learned over time that my mom's judgement of her capability was not always in sync with reality.

My mom was convinced there was nothing wrong with her and that she could take a shower on her own. Each time the paid caregiver would ask mom, "Can I help you with changing and showering?" she would respond with a firm NO. I tried several times to gently offer, "Mom, can I please help you with your shower, it really would make me feel better." Even after the grab bars were installed, she would fall occasionally while changing her clothes. After an unpleasant fall, we finally got her to agree to leave the door a little open so we could hear her when she needed help.

My mom finally allowed me to help her in the shower with shampoo, soap and conditioner. I was guaranteed two showers on those days ☺.

Finally, when my mom was completely bedridden, I was amazed with the skills and strength of the person that came through Hospice by the Sea to bathe my mom. Hospice by the Sea is a non-profit that provides palliative care and support to the family at the residence of the patient. If mom was awake, she almost always wanted to get out of bed and take a shower. However, at the end she was mostly getting dry showers. My mom was very lucky to have someone as skilled as Julie to give her dry showers and keep her clean and bedsore-free. I marveled at Julie's skills when one day I watched her change my mom's clothes, give her a dry shower, brush her teeth, change her bed sheets, and cut her nails, all while my mom stayed fast asleep.

Slapping Someone

Ruby

It's still shocking to me, that my sweet mom slapped someone.

When I heard from the caregivers at the assisted living facility that my mom was arguing with them and slapping them, I said, "That is just not possible. My mom has never yelled at anyone her whole life, how could she possibly slap someone?" Upon further investigation, I found out that she had been sleepwalking. When my mom would sleepwalk, she would take on a completely different personality. She would become loud, argumentative and would slap anyone that tried to take her back to her room.

This started when my dad was hospitalized for a few days. I ended up moving my mom to live with me while dad was in the hospital. I just could not imagine letting her suffer with sleepwalking like that. I felt devastated to see the change in her personality.

Abuse Investigation

Ruby

I felt relieved that even though there are a lot of incidents of elder abuse, my mom was certainly not experiencing it.

I did research on elder abuse when my parents were in assisted living and my mom was complaining about caregivers at that facility. She claimed that they were pushing her and holding her too tight. After further investigation, I found out that she had started sleepwalking again and was trying to leave the facility at night.

The caregivers had to stop her in her tracks and take her back to her room. She showed no signs of physical abuse and my dad witnessed a few interactions and tried to intervene. Even though he was over protective of her, his feeling was that her claims were unfounded. If he wasn't worried, I had no reason to worry.

Pain Management Based on Judgment

Ruby

My mom was unable to effectively communicate the level of pain she was experiencing, making it difficult for us to administer the right doses of pain medications.

Pain management was a tough challenge as there was no way for me to measure mom's pain while she was sleeping or moving her legs restlessly.

My mom always under-estimated her pain, even though you could see from her facial expression and her moans that she was in pain. She would also scream in anguish while sleeping. It was especially difficult to assess whether it was emotional distress due to a nightmare or physical pain. This situation felt like watching my mom being tortured but not being able to see by whom and how. The best I could do was to have medications on hand to address physical pain and anxiety. I also had a muscle relaxant that was prescribed for times we saw her kicking her legs in restlessness. With these three medications and recommended doses at my disposal, I had to figure out by trial and error how to keep my mom comfortable. Sometimes she was peaceful within an hour following the administration of the meds, while at other times it took up to sixteen hours to get her relaxed.

Identifying and Taking Action Against Abuse

Mariya

Lisa was able to find community resources to step in to tackle a tough situation.

Lisa's aunt was being physically abused by the caregiver her daughter-in-law had hired. Her son and daughter-in-law did not want to be called negligent for their hiring of what they said was "a carefully chosen caregiver". So, her daughter-in-law kept making excuses about her aunt's bruises. When Lisa's mom moved in with the aunt, Lisa and her mom decided to take action.

Lisa searched online for government resources on senior abuse. She found a number to call for a state authority and called it to report the situation, knowing full well that it would probably destroy any remnants of her relationship with her cousin. The next day an investigator showed up at her aunt's doorstep. Her cousin happened to be in town and working from home that day. The investigator was a true professional. He assessed the situation very quickly. By doing a background check on the caregiver he found out that she had prior reports of elder abuse. He asked Lisa's mom, "Do you want me to handle all communications and arrangements with your nephew?"

"Yes please," her mom nodded with a sigh.

The investigator not only got her cousin to fire the caregiver immediately, but he was also able to arrange for two weeks of paid respite care while they found another caregiver.

The next day Lisa received a call from her cousin saying, "I know you and your mom conspired and called local authorities. You are not here in person, and do not know everything. If your mom wants to continue to live here, this going behind our backs better not happen again." Lisa was neither surprised nor rattled by the call. She simply knew that it was necessary to grow a thick skin in order to care for her seenagers.

Treasure Hunting in Unexpected Places

Noah & Aliya

Lisa felt that a treasure hunt was essential to having necessary funds for her parents growing needs.

Finding all the places where financial resources might be hidden was not easy for Lisa. It was important to go on a hunting trip for various potential assets while her seenagers were still able to help with the process of accessing passwords, locating the names of institutions, etc.

Long-Term Savings

Lisa's dad liked investing in a variety of things and over the years had invested in bonds and annuities that he had completely forgotten about. Lisa discovered this treasure when she was going through eleven boxes of his financial paperwork after she got the Financial Power of Attorney. She had been tempted to just throw away everything in those boxes as the task of sifting through the paperwork seemed tedious. It was a good thing that her dad made her promise to do a careful review of paperwork before shredding. She discovered $50,000 worth of bonds.

Retirement Plans

When Lisa and my seenagers were working they were enrolled in pension plans. We had looked at each of our seenager's work history and investigated what pensions they had coming to them. Each of our seenagers readily recalled the names of companies they had worked for a long period of time, but several of the companies where they worked for a short period of time were not shared with us. Without the benefit of Internet, let alone LinkedIn we may have left some funds undiscovered. One day when Lisa and her dad were at a doctor's office. Her dad bumped into a colleague of his from a company he had failed to mention earlier, so she made a note to follow up with that company. Turned out that her dad had invested in an employee stock option plan at that company. This resulted in another $10,000.

Collector's Treasure

Lisa's mom was a collector like her husband, but instead of collecting investments, she collected artificial jewelry, fur coats and teacups. Lisa and her mom had meticulously tagged who should receive what in case of her death. She had over one hundred people on that list. When Lisa needed money to pay for her mom's care at the end of her life, Lisa decided to sell some of the expensive fur coats to pay for it. Her mom was sad about the decision but gave her approval.

Bank accounts

Lisa was able to help her parents find checking accounts that they had opened over the years and had forgotten. Her mom had opened an account to save for a trip around the world. As her health deteriorated she gave up on that idea and told Lisa about that account.

Emotional Abuse Can Hurt Too

Aliya

Lisa found that emotional abuse from her cousins was impacting her mom's well-being.

Lisa could sense a further decline in her mom's emotional well-being, after her cousins hired a new caregiver to replace the one that was abusing her aunt. It did not make sense to Lisa why her mom seemed unusually depressed. After coaxing her mom to share, Lisa found out that the new caregiver was required to provide an overly detailed daily status report on her aunt and mom to her cousin and his wife. The caregiver was also listening in on her mom's conversations over the phone and eavesdropping on conversations when her mom had any visitors. One day, Lisa's mom was confronted angrily by her cousin and his wife.

"I understand that you had a conversation with your niece in Seattle and that you were talking about what you eat. We don't think it's anyone else's business what happens in this household. We don't want you to have such conversations." Her mom felt that not only was she walking on egg shells and was under twenty-four hours of surveillance, but she was being talked down to on a regular basis.

Lisa got very concerned and felt helpless, she wished her mom had friends locally that could take her out of the house and be her confidants.

While doing research on the web, Lisa found the "age-in-place" senior village in the area. As it turned out, the Executive Director of the Village was a neighbor and friend of her cousin. Right after the ED's first visit with Lisa's mom, her cousin's attitude changed. There was no way he was going to have his dirty laundry aired in public. Things became superficially pleasant and that was good enough for her mom.

My Sleep is More Important than Yours

Aliya & Noah

Lisa has always wondered if not having a good night's sleep and suffering with sleep apnea contributed to her dad's decline in health.

Lisa's mom and dad had fought for years about who snored the loudest. They made an agreement that they would both go for a sleep study at the same time. It turned out that they both had sleep apnea, but mom's apnea was worse than dad's. Dad told mom, "This proves you snore louder than me, I was right all along. You need to get the CPAP machine."

Her mom decided, "If I get one, I want it to be small so I can use it while we travel. When we are home I will sleep in the other bedroom." Neither Lisa nor the doctors could convince them to use the CPAP machine on a regular basis, even by saying things like, "You will sleep better… wake up more rested… have a better quality of life… along with lots of other preventative health benefits." They both thought the mask looked very uncomfortable. Lisa's only hope was that if mom started using it she would see the benefit, and would want to use it daily. But after a while, Lisa gave up on the argument and did not bring it up.

When Lisa's mom moved in with her sister, their bedrooms were not only connected, the walls seemed to be very thin. She decided to try out the CPAP machine to avoid waking up Aunt Mariya.

"Lisa, I can't tell you how rested I feel. This thing works. The first few days were not comfortable, getting used to the mask etc.... but the last couple of nights have been awesome," her mom said to Lisa a week later.

Over the years, Lisa tried to convince her dad that he should consider using a CPAP machine. But as his health declined, pain increased and memory started to go, getting him to try something new became so much more difficult.

Overmedicated

Noah

Lisa thought controlling pain medication was cruel, until she saw news segments on opioid addiction and consulted with her dad's physician.

Lisa's dad wanted to control his meds and had a habit of frequently overdosing, including his intake of prescription pain medicines. Lisa and her dad would have big fights over it, as he would sleep for twenty to thirty hours straight after an overdose. She started rationing his medicine. She thought she had worked out a fool-proof system. However, he had asked a friend to mail him his leftover painkillers from surgery. He was using them to supplement the rationed dosage Lisa was giving him.

It took a couple of weeks for Lisa to figure out what he was doing. Lisa then looked for a medication management solution. She found one that could give her alerts when he used the meds, but dad would not have anything to do with that. Finally, after negotiations for several weeks, they agreed upon a week-long pillbox. It had four compartments for each day, that made it easier for Lisa to casually go in his room and see if he had taken more meds than needed on any given day. She then removed all other medication bottles from his room. Less was never her worry.

Props When You Need Them

Noah

Lisa found it surprising to learn that canes come with special features in base, handle, weight and size adjustments.

As Lisa's dad's walk started to look wobbly, she decided it would be a good idea to get him a cane. The day after she got him a cane, she watched him pick up the cane that slipped from his hands. She felt mortified as he stumbled to the ground in the process of picking up the dropped cane.

Lisa went to the AARP website to see if they had a recommendation. She found a post by Alejandra Owens on "Hazardous Walking? Beware!" that said "Nearly 50,000 older Americans fall each year as a result of improperly measured/fitted canes and walkers, we have to stop and wonder what we can do to fix this problem. Simply stated – talk to your doctor or physical therapist."

She also found information on one that was called HurryCane. This cane keeps standing straight even when you leave it. She immediately went to the nearby drug store and bought it for him even before her planned discussion with his physical therapist. This cane seemed to be working well for him. However, when they finally visited a physical therapist he helped adjust the height for better comfort and safety.

Climbing Stairs Challenge

Noah

Lisa had to look for new solutions to help her dad as his condition worsened.

Lisa's home had an office on the first floor but not a full bath. Her first solution was to get a chair lift installed on her steps, so her dad could go upstairs to take a bath. They used that solution until her dad started experiencing dementia. One day as he was going down the steps on his chair, he decided to get off the chair a few steps before he had reached the bottom. He tumbled to the floor and broke his already weakened knee. He ended up in ER, hospital and eventually a nursing home for a couple of months.

This gave Lisa time to expand their downstairs bathroom. Lisa got guidance from a local non-profit that focused on fall prevention. With their recommendation, she put in a big walk-in shower, and moved the laundry room into the basement. The shower had slightly slanted floor so that water would not go out of the shower. It also had a big enough door to roll in a wheelchair and a custom seat. Lisa thinks that this one expense saved them significant dollars in caregiver costs for his bathing needs, and kept him independent for much longer. That truly was priceless.

Summary

Lisa and I both had our patience tested beyond our limits. We found ourselves struggling emotionally, and we both became more irritable and easily frustrated while going through these challenges.

However, we both believe that we are much stronger people for having gone through these experiences.

Chapter 6 – Taking Their Independence

Their Loss of Independence Created Ripples in All Our Lives

Whether we were taking car keys away from our seenagers or moving them to a new home, there were times in our journeys as caregivers when we had to take our loved ones' independence away from them. The sacrifice of freedom for security was really difficult.

I remember someone saying to me, "It was so difficult to take my mom's car keys away." At the time, I judged these people and thought, "Just remind them of the numerous accidents and fatalities caused by seniors. That should be enough to scare anyone." Looking back, I know I was over simplifying and not taking into account her mom's feelings.

I am going to fight you
If you tell me what to do.
I am still me
Do not tell me what I cannot do.

Driving Privileges Equals Manliness

Jay & Sami

When I thought of taking away Independence, I thought losing driving privileges would be the hardest one for men – and it was.

I was shocked with the amount of resistance I received by my two male seenagers when I talked to them about giving up their car keys. After lots of hits and misses, I finally learned that I had to be better prepared to address all of their concerns and emotions before I brought up the subject seriously. This was not a "one-time discussion" by any means.

I can never forget the despair in my uncle's eyes the day he finally agreed to give up his car keys.

"You are taking away my manliness," he told me.

There was nothing I could say to make him feel better, other than, "You are and always will be an amazing man and my favorite uncle."

For both my uncle and my dad I had to find other means of transportation. For my uncle, I found a cab service that had contracted with the state to provide discounted cab rides to seniors. For my parents, I found a Jewish Family Services option called "Rides and Smiles" that provided free transportation as long as it was booked seven days in advance. I believe that new transportation services and self-driving cars are eventually going to make this discussion easier. I wish I had these solutions at my disposal for my seenagers.

Loss of Independent Mobility

Ruby

Loss of independent mobility was confusing for my mom.

After my dad passed away and my mom moved back in with me, it became very difficult to take care of her. My mom was unable to move without assistance. She needed help to get up from a sitting position most of the time. Once in a while she would surprise us by getting up on her own when no one was looking. She could not call out for help because her vocal cords had been affected by Parkinson's resulting in such a soft speech that one could barely hear her event sitting next to her. We installed an alarm system that would buzz anytime she would get out of bed or when her feet would touch the floor. We also had a little buzzer around her neck that she just had to press to sound an alarm so that someone in the house could go to her aid immediately. All that worked for a while, but it wore down the entire family, as the alarm sounds were loud and obnoxious.

Eventually we decided to get rid of that method and installed a Nest monitor which sends a text message anytime there is motion or noise detected in specific part of the house. One day, I was upstairs when I heard the doorbell ring. Mom heard it too and suddenly decided to go open the door. She made it all the way from her bed to the door, only to fall two steps away from her destination. The text I received was slightly delayed in reaching my phone and resulted in a fall for mom.

However, with a big bruise on her hip, I decided we had no choice left but to get round-the-clock care.

Leave Me Alone

Ruby

"You can leave me alone, I don't need a babysitter," is something I heard frequently from my mom as she defied the need for having round the clock caregiver.

My mom had random episodes of dementia. She would sleep twenty out of twenty-four hours every day. The four hours a day she was awake weren't continuous and worse yet were during random times of the day and night. When she got up she needed help in pretty much all of the activities of daily living, including bathing, transferring from her chair or bed, physical hygiene, meal preparation and medicine management. It was impossible to leave mom alone. Even after the fall where she bruised her hip. She would keep insisting, "I don't need someone to babysit me all day long. You can leave me alone."

At first, I lied to my mom about the caretakers I had hired to provide round the clock care for her. I told her that I had hired several people to help me around the house, so she should not be alarmed if she saw a stranger in her room helping her. She never questioned that excuse, as when she was a child her parents always had hired housekeepers and gardeners. This little white lie allowed my mom to accept her caregivers.

Grieving the Loss of Independence

Sami

It surprising to see my uncle follow the stages of grief sequentially for loss of his independence, since most people don't.

Psychologist Kubler Ross defines the five stages of grief as being anger, denial, bargaining, depression and acceptance. When my uncle began facing the loss of his own independence, he illustrated these five stages perfectly and in the right order. Whenever the safety or security of my uncle was threatened, or he reached a new low, I saw him go through these stages in this order. At times, he went through the stages within hours, while other times, it took him months.

Denial

My uncle was convinced that I or the doctor just had to be wrong about his condition and he would cling to a preferable reality instead.

"There is no way I need to take this medication for the rest of my life. I will take it for a month. I'll get better and then stop it."

Anger

My uncle was well-known in the family for his anger, and some of his bouts with anger would leave me shaking in my boots. I heard him scream things like: "How can this happen to me? Who is to blame?" I also saw him punch and kick furniture when he was angry.

Bargaining

My uncle would then ask me to look for other options to fix the situation. He would try to negotiate relentlessly with me or the doctor to find alternatives or compromises. When he was going through this stage, the demand on my time were unreasonably high. He would call me and say, "I just read this on the Internet. Can you call your friend Dr. Paul and ask him about this procedure? Also, could you look at these websites? I don't know how to use forums well. Can you post these questions on the site for me? Can you call the drug company and ask them about these side effects?"

He would end his long list of "to-dos" for me with this statement, "I know I am on to something here. If I do these things, I am sure I can negotiate with my doctor about not being on these drugs. You will see, I will be fine without them."

Depression

Once, my uncle figured out that there was no bargaining out of his health crisis and that he had to resign to a new reality for his body, he then became silent, refused visitors, stopped taking my calls and spent much of the time mournful and sullen. Many times, I took a flight to see him only to be told, "What was the point in coming and wasting your vacation and hard-earned money? I'm going to die soon!" or he would start a long “poor me” monologue that inevitably began with "I miss the way …"

Acceptance

Once, my uncle and I were successful in riding out the other stages, and getting him to acceptance, I was then able to provide him with required assistance for his changed condition. This included the loss of yet another level of independence but he would typically be calm, gain a retrospective view, and be emotionally stable.

Loss of Financial Control

Sami

Looking back, I know now that he could sense the time was near, and he was not keeping up with his finances in a way he would like.

My uncle shocked me one day by handing me access and control of his well-organized financial files and keys to everything he owned. After years of penny-pinching and hording money all of his life, he handed me the keys to his kingdom, one month prior to his death. Even though things were meticulously organized he had not created a will nor had he made any decisions on what should be done with his wealth once he passed.

He had also not been able to pay any of his bills for months and there were several collection notices. He had decided to go for unnecessary medical procedures for weight loss against his physician's advice. Some of these procedures were not covered by insurance. He also had made some investments using his home equity loan. Even though his home was paid off, the bill was past due in paying the home equity loan. Needless to say, his finances were a mess and the younger, more successful version of himself as a Chief Financial Officer would not have believed he would be in a position like this by the end of his life.

I spent hours on the phone cleaning up his various past due bills, debts and collection notices.

I also found an attorney to help him create a Will, so he could decide what to do with his wealth, decisions I did not want to make on his behalf.

Incontinence Is a Loss

Noah

Lisa's dad considered forced help for incontinence issues as another loss of independence.

When Lisa said that we should put incontinence as one of the topics in the chapter on "taking independence away" from the seenagers, I argued against it at first. However, when she explained how her dad reacted to the discussion about incontinence, I knew that she was right. "What do you mean by that, are you saying that I cannot be trusted to take care of my own bodily functions?" Lisa's dad reacted angrily.

With strong outbursts on her father's part, Lisa knew she needed some advice and guidance on how to tackle this issue. Late that night she sent a text message to a friend who worked at a room-and-board facility for seniors. She got a text back the next morning, "We use the website shopdependabledaughter, they are great, they will walk you through the options you have based on your dad's condition."

After a thorough discussion with the representative from the company, Lisa felt prepared to have a talk with her dad again.

“Dad, I talked to someone today about some things you can do to make your life easier. You get up, shower, change and get dressed so nicely every morning. Don’t you want to feel fresh all day?”

Knowing full well that Lisa was going to sweet talk him into something that he may not be very happy about doing, her dad nodded with a smile. The fact was that he really had no other choice.

“Dad, there are these adult briefs we can get for you, so that even if you have an accident you don’t have to take a shower and change your clothes again. If you are okay with that, I will order some for you.”

Even though she knew it would improve her father’s quality of life, Lisa felt badly that she had just tricked her dad. Adult briefs are essentially adult diapers. It took a couple of weeks for her dad to completely accept this change in his life, but when he finally did, he told Lisa, “You were right, it is great to have these new briefs and not to have to change my clothes and take a second shower.”

He would promptly remind Lisa to call Dependable Daughter at least a week in advance of him running out of his new briefs. Figuring out how to preserve dignity in these situations was hard but doable.

Declared Incompetent

Noah

Lisa remembers the day when her dad was declared incompetent as the day the tables turned in their relationship. She was now officially his protector.

Lisa's dad had been a gambler for many years. When he moved in with her, Lisa began getting calls on her home phone from collection agencies. At first, she ignored the calls or if they would say it was for her dad, she would just hand over the phone to him. When these calls became incessant, she sat down with him and forced him to finally tell her what was going on. She was amazed to find out that her dad was not able to explain the state of his finances in a coherent manner. That was so unlike him, with the amount of public speaking he had done all his life, she had never imagined him not be able to get his point across.

Lisa then started to listen in on the other line to some of the calls he was getting and found him not much different with the collection agencies. One time she heard him yelling really loudly at a collection agency and after he hung up, she saw him with his hand on his heart. She asked him "are you okay dad?" He was visibly in pain and not able to breathe. She called 911. In the ER, the doctor told her that her dad had suffered an anxiety attack.

Lisa then got advice from another friend who had been through something similar. Her friend told her, "You have got to get your dad declared incompetent and take over for him as a conservator."

Lisa realized after a week with her dad back at home that his mental condition was not stable enough for him to handle any of his affairs. Lisa agonized for several weeks on how to approach her dad. She started by slowly dropping hints and using words like "conservator" in her conversations with him. She would say, "Dad, let me take care of this for you as your conservator." After hearing her use the word several times, he asked her to explain what the word meant. "It just means that I am your #1 helper, dad." This was true and it allowed Lisa's dad to agree to this new arrangement.

Having set the stage with dad, she had to quickly go through the process of getting him declared incompetent and officially become his conservator. She could not take care of any of his affairs without the official document.

This was not a one-hour process; it took time and required several steps. Lisa had to go to court, luckily with her dad's consent. A court investigator was assigned to interview her dad. A hearing was held with an investigator and a judge who in turn appointed her as a conservator to manage her dad's affairs. While going through the process Lisa was focused on getting herself appointed in that role, but the moment the judge declared her dad incompetent, Lisa broke down into tears. She admitted to her husband, "This is one case I wish I was proven wrong, and lost." That day, Lisa had to begin mourning the dad who had protected her all of her life and realized she was now his protector.

Lisa was declared her dad's conservator only for his "estate" (meaning financial affairs) at that time. She was not given the right to oversee his daily activities, his health care or living arrangements.

Summary

We learned the hard way that our concerns for the safety and security of our seenagers were not always shared readily by them. They argued with us for as long as they could about the decline in their condition. They also had strong opinions about the possible negative impacts on their lives.

The "taking independence away" conversations were truly difficult and multifaceted. The complexities arose because we shared the feeling of loss with our seenagers. In addition, their safety and security impacted everyone around them. Plus, we had to learn new processes or tools and accept a change in lifestyle.

Many of the tested techniques for convincing others to change their behaviors worked with my seenagers, with various levels of success. I tried the "carrot stick" method I had used with my kids. "If you agree not to drive, I will take you on the vacation of your dreams."

I put up metaphorical guard rails much like I had done with my babies. For example: I set the Nest monitor to text me when they moved out of bed.

I even tried the proven Fear, Uncertainty, and Doubt approach (FUD) used in business sales like, "If you continue to drive, you may kill someone like the situation we just heard about in Los Angeles. I can't imagine how badly that senior must feel knowing they have taken some young lives." I felt like a monster anytime I was desperate and used the FUD factor approach, as I was frightening my already scared and vulnerable seenager.

I finally figured out my most successful approach which focused on first helping them with the grief of their loss of independence. Saying things like the following really helped: "I am so sorry to have to bring up the subject of driving. I know that is something that you really enjoy. I know that it makes you feel independent. I know that it will be very sad for you and even for me to see you not be able to drive again. It will be a loss. However, we have to address this new reality we find ourselves in."

There was rarely a time when taking away independence was a "one discussion decision." Most of the time there were several discussions on the same subject, before we could all see eye to eye.

As my seenagers lost their independence, I gained more responsibilities. The more responsibilities I gained, the more my personal life, my other relationships, health, and work, were impacted. However, in hindsight, the tasks that were added to our plate were far easier than the dramatic risks we avoided. The old adage, “prevention is better than cure,” was certainly applicable here.

Chapter 7 – Leveraging Legal Documents

Taking Our Head Out of the Sand and Facing Legal Documents

All of my adult life, I despised anything having to do with legal documents. When I bought my first house on my own, I remember the real estate agent telling me to read the contract carefully. I took this process very seriously and spent a full weekend reading through every word. After that weekend, I never wanted to read another legal document ever again.

Being a caregiver however has taught me that some of these legal documents can be as helpful as angels guiding you in a crisis.

Lisa and I used different documents based on what we knew and what law required in the states we were in. We found that the names of the document may differ from state to state or country to country, but overall the kinds of issues that these legal documents address are the same.

Healthcare Power of Attorney

Alli & Sami

This document gave me the authority to take decisions on their behalf regarding their healthcare. It was a power I wish I did not need to have.

I needed healthcare power of attorney for all my seenagers because there came a time in each of their journeys when they were not able to make healthcare decisions on their own.

I had struggled with my aunt's healthcare decisions because she did not have a POA. Therefore, when I created my parents POA, I prepared it using a very comprehensive template. I also prepared those well ahead of time and made the tough decisions jointly with my parents while we were not in a crisis.

I really did not want to create a healthcare POA for my hard to please uncle because we just did not see eye-to-eye on these matters. Our opinions differed on almost everything including when to change treatment to palliative care. I asked my uncle's stepdaughter to step into that role. She did initially when the document was being prepared but as soon as both of them signed the document, she changed her mind and as I was the backup responsibilities fell on me. Once that happened, I asked my uncle's most trusted friend to have joint signature on a new POA, since I felt I needed someone else as a buffer in case his step daughter changed her mind again.

These were only a few things that were in my uncle's health POA. He was very specific and very prescriptive about situations that would be of deep interest to him, such as:

- Save his life if he is unconscious.
- The doctor has permission to remove a limb.
- Any invasive or experimental surgery even with the highest risks is permissible in all circumstances.
- If he gets dementia, adjust his medication dosage to the highest possible levels to minimize dementia even if it increases the risk to his life.

Once the POAs were in place, I made copies for all applicable parties: doctors, hospitals, or nursing facilities. I also emailed it to any family members who might be interested in voicing their opinion and influencing the decisions, if they so choose.

Advance Directive

Jay & Ruby

The advance directive form was provided to us when my dad ended up in the hospital.

This document covered most of the same things that the healthcare power of attorney did, and provided a place to officially name me as his "health care agent."

There were things in the advance directive that were not as concisely spelled out in the healthcare POA. So, we discussed various situations where I may need to make decisions for their healthcare for life-sustaining procedures in the event of a terminal condition, persistent vegetative state or end-stage condition.

Physician Orders for Life-Sustaining Treatment

Ruby

Not giving life sustaining oxygen to my mom... What a cruel choice I was forced to make.

On the day that my passed away, we were moving her to a nursing home. The paramedics asked if she had a Physician Orders for Life-Sustaining Treatment (POLST, a standard document in California), as they were carrying her into the ambulance. The POLST form is a doctor's medical order indicating a patient's wishes regarding treatments that are commonly used in a medical crisis. My mom had a healthcare POA, an advance directive and a POLST document. The EMT specifically asked for a copy of the POLST form.

Even though I had a healthcare POA for my mom and she also had an advanced directive, emergency medical technicians (EMTs) and hospitals staff are required to follow emergency medical protocols unless doctor's orders say otherwise. Even if resuscitation or other end-of-life preferences are specified in any other document, they can't be honored without the POLST form, at least in California.

Before they started driving the ambulance, they told me that her pulse was extremely week and her breath was shallow. They asked me if they should put an oxygen mask on her. Recalling the advice of her physician that prolonging her life at this stage is adding to her suffering, I declined. It was the most difficult NO of my life.

She stopped breathing in the ambulance, and the EMT had physician's orders in hand telling them what not to do at that time.

Death with Dignity (DWD)

Sami

With the Death with Dignity (a.k.a. Dignity Statutes) Document, my uncle defined when he wanted his life to end.

My uncle liked to control things, and I am not surprised that he asked me to investigate the dignity statues document. I had not heard about this document until my uncle asked me to look into it. What I found was that DWD is about deliberately ending life whereas POLST is about how people want to live and be cared for with their serious illness or frailty. The DWD document would allow my uncle to clearly state his wishes regarding the ways to end his life in the event of either unbearable pain or of being in a coma.

My uncle told me with highest level of secrecy, that he had found the right doctor, one that had YES to a very important question. With a puzzled look in my eyes I asked my uncle "what was that so very important question?"

He responded "If I were terminally ill and wanted to use California End of Life Option Act, would you be willing to write me a prescription for life ending medication?"

Financial Power of Attorney (POA)

Sami

I was completely shocked when my uncle gave to me the "keys to the kingdom" and allowed me to control his finances entirely.

He also had an attorney friend of his prepare a financial POA. This was very comprehensive in providing me POA for any and all of his financial matters. This POA gave me access to his bank account and the authority to make changes to his accounts, including his safe deposit, real estate dealings, investments, and valuable collections. I found out that banks look very carefully at these documents and it was great that the POA was detailed enough for the bank.

It also included a clause for granting POA to things he may have failed to identify in this POA. Needless to say, his stepdaughter was not too happy about any of this, but there was nothing she could do.

Will for Life and After Death

Sami

My uncle's attorney claimed he had the most complicated will he had ever seen. My uncle could have created a simple one, but that was not his style.

He wanted his monetary and other worldly possessions distributed to various individuals and non-profits. For many of those to be collected, there were certain criteria the individual or non-profit had to meet. For example, his stepdaughter had to be present for his funeral and his first-year death anniversary celebration, if she was going to see a dime of his money.

A local non-profit could only collect on their share of the inheritance if they had $100,000 in assets. His attorney explained that, "He wanted this non-profit to be financially solvent if they were going to receive any money from his will." The only person in his will that did not have to meet any criteria was me. His gesture validated for me that he appreciated what I had done as a caregiver for him.

I was certainly glad that he had made his attorney friend the executor of his will and not me.

Living Wills Defined Terms for Living

Aliya & Noah

Lisa's parents both had living wills that documented their wishes in writing in case they were unable to make decisions for themselves.

Lisa also had healthcare POAs for her parents. However, she found out while making decisions about her dad's care (when he was unable to speak for himself) that his living will trumped the healthcare POA.

When her mom's physical condition reached a point of no return, Lisa knew that putting her mom on a feeding tube and ventilator would just prolong her suffering, and that was against her mom's wishes. Lisa had submitted the living will, which her mom had put together many years ago when she was much younger, to thc hospital the day she was admitted. The problem however, was that her living will clearly stated that she should be kept alive using a ventilator and artificially supplied nutrition if necessary. Also, her living will did not document what measures should be taken at the end of her life to keep her comfortable.

Lisa wished that she had the living will amended with her mom's latest wishes, while her mom was still able to make decisions. So, when the hospital put her mom on a ventilator, Lisa's only recourse was to make sure she was given enough morphine to keep her comfortable. She passed away after being on a ventilator for two weeks. The anguish of seeing her mom in pain totally eclipsed the financial challenges of keeping her alive on the ventilator. It was truly an overwhelming situation for her.

Representative Payee for Managing Social Security

Aliya

Lisa's mom had to become a representative payee to manage her dad's Social Security benefits.

Lisa found out even though her father was declared incompetent, that she did not automatically have the rights to manage his Social Security benefits. She could not change addresses, redirect the payment to a new bank account or get reports. For Lisa's mom to be a representative payee she had to apply and be appointed by the Social Security Administration (SSA). The SSA did not accept financial POA documents in-lieu of the representative payee documentation. Once she was approved, she was able to make sure his checks were getting properly deposited into their bank account on a monthly basis.

HIPAA Authorization Needed for Medical Records

Aliya

Lisa needed the Health Insurance Portability and Accountability Act (HIPAA) authorization signed by her mom to get a copy of her medical records.

HIPAA protects the privacy and security of health information.

When Lisa's mom was going to move to live with her Aunt Mariya, her medical records had to be transferred to her new doctors. Lisa found out that she could not pick-up any medical records for her mom from the physician's office or the hospital in Missouri until both Lisa and her mom had signed a HIPAA authorization form.

Even though Lisa had a medical POA it was not enough to get her medical records.

Summary

Lisa and I agree that knowing what we know now, we would prepare these documents while our seenagers were coherent, so we would not have to deal with having to make tough decisions in the midst of a crisis without being able to have input from them.

Chapter 8 – Captaining Their Transition

Ironic How Having Nearly Total Control Seemed So Wrong

All through the caregiving journey, we would get frustrated when our seenagers didn't want to listen to our recommendations. We thought we knew better most of the time, and if only they would listen to us, their circumstances would become easier. However, in this phase of caregiving, our seenagers were really not able to argue with us. It truly is ironic, how when we got what we wanted, it was just too overwhelming to handle.

Hospice Care

Ruby

At the end of mom's life, we chose hospice care at home for my mom, so that we could singularly focus on keeping her comfortable, rather than curing her.

When my mom reached a stage when she no longer wanted any more treatment for her ailments, and just wanted to be kept comfortable, I learned all the words that represented her stage of care: *palliative care, hospice care and comfort care*. Her primary care and neurologist both agreed that there was nothing they could do to treat her condition and that she should be moved to hospice care. However, when the provider's palliative care organization sent someone to evaluate if my mom's condition was suitable for hospice care, he declined to accept her into the palliative care program. Their reasoning was that she could live a long time in that condition, and in that case the insurance would not reimburse them for the coverage.

I called my friend Judy who had worked as a hospice social worker for many years. I asked her, "Have you ever heard of a case where someone's primary care physician, their specialist, the patient and family all agree that the patient should now get palliative care, but hospice care provider refuses to accept the patient?"

"Unfortunately, yes," she said. "But you know you can call another Hospice agency and see what they think. I have a friend that is a physician for Hospice by the Sea. Call them tomorrow and see what they say."

They sent the most amazing and compassionate physician to my home to assess my mom's condition. After a thorough review of my mom's condition he said, "I agree with your mom's physician. Your mom does not have very long to live and she should be considered a hospice patient and only be provided palliative care. There is really no cure for her condition, and there are really no drugs that will prolong her life. I would allow her to eat what she wants, and don't wake her up to give her medications. You understand that palliative care is comfort care. So, we will do whatever it takes to keep her comfortable." He added, "I will tell you this though, that sometimes when we accept a patient into hospice and they are feeling comfortable, they start doing better. When we start focusing on your mom's comfort, she will start to enjoy her days, and she may even smile more."

I was feeling a huge sense of grief at the thought of losing my mom soon, but I was also feeling a sense of relief that I would not be feeling obligated to take my mom for tests, doctor visits or ER if she was not doing well. As my mom's health declined, we continued to adjust the dosage of morphine and other drugs to keep her comfortable.

Since the cost of a professional caregiver or hospice facility is mostly an out-of-pocket expense, we decided to do hospice at home for my mom. I would have felt like I was abandoning my mom when she needed me the most at the end of her life if I had moved her to a hospice facility.

The hospice services that were made available for her were occasional visits from the doctor, social worker and chaplain, along with home delivery of medications. More importantly, there were weekly visits from a nurse and someone who came to bathe my mom every day of the week.

I had to hire round-the-clock caregivers to essentially sit and watch my mom sleep for ninety-nine percent of the time. She would sometimes sleep for days and then wake up at an odd hour needing to use the restroom. We would force her to eat or drink and give her meds when she would wake up. Given that my mom needed coverage seven days a week, twenty-four hours a day, I hired eleven caregivers during a nine-month period.

It was hard to find someone willing to do that, even when the majority of the time there was nothing to do. I hired students, people looking for a place to live, people looking for a second job, and a mom and daughter duo. The reason for the high turnover was that I could not pay them as much as they could make somewhere else. I remember saying, “I know you are worth lot more, but this is what I can afford. I can give you room, food and let you use my car, but I cannot afford to give you a higher wage.”

A few months into it I had found out about a county program that pays vetted providers little less than $10/hour directly. My mom had to get approved for the program. They approved fifteen hours a week, which was by no means enough. I fought the ruling that was based on a visit by a county assessor. I really felt that she had some sort of bias against us when she told me at the end of her visit, “Your mom looks fine and I don’t understand why you need someone around to help her get out of a chair. Just get her a walker.” I tried explaining to her that given my mom’s Parkinson’s disease, a walker would not work because she does not have enough strength to lift herself up, to lean on a walker, or worse yet to prevent a fall when she freezes.

After going in front of a county judge with this case, my mom was given 270 hours a month of support. It was still not enough to cover the over 720 hours a month needed, but it certainly helped.

The difficult part was finding someone that was county approved to provide the service. Some of the challenges included: availability, willingness to drive to my home, willingness to just sit and watch my mom sleep. Luckily, the savings account my brother and I had set aside a long time ago helped in paying for these expenses.

Respite Care

Ruby

Short but sweet respite care for my mom, allowed me to take care of my other obligations.

A few months after my father's death, while my mom was living with me, I had an urgent business trip come up. Unfortunately, neither my boss not my peers could attend the meeting in my place. As we were walking into a meeting, my boss suggested I call 211 to see if there was a local non-profit that could help with respite care. I had never heard of 211. At first, I thought that she meant to say 411 for directory assistance. However, as I was walking to my meeting I dialed 211, someone with the name Jacob picked up the phone. I told Jacob, "I am running into a meeting but I wanted to know if there are any local companies that can provide respite care for my mom while I am on a business trip."

Jacob responded in a very kind and calm voice, "Since you are in a rush, if you give me your email address, I will send you a list in a few minutes." A few minutes later as I was sitting in the meeting I saw an email magically appear in my inbox with a list of providers, along with their contact information and their description.

I called the first one on the list: Southern Caregiver Resource Center (SCRC), and shared with them my situation. I was amazed when the lady told me that she could help me. “Let me schedule a time for a case worker to meet you and your mom,” she told me sweetly. I was concerned about cost and worried the service would be unaffordable.

“What will the cost be for a week?” I asked her.

“No cost to you. SCRC funds respite services to relieve caregivers of the stresses of constant care. Respite is designed to provide care to a loved one for a brief period of time so the caregiver has the opportunity to address any challenges they may be facing, including time to just rest. We have contracts with select, professional agencies to provide this service at your home.” I couldn’t believe there really was such a service free of charge to me.

A couple of months later, I was able to travel with a lot less worries on my plate.

Preventing Bedsores

Ruby

Mom's hospice team had warned us about how painful bedsores (a.k.a. pressure ulcers) can be, and how slow they are to heal. The best thing to prevent them was not letting mom be in one position for extended periods of time.

My mom slept for about twenty hours a day for a few years before she went into a coma. As time went on, her sleeping episodes kept getting longer. On several occasions during the last five months of life, she slept for several days straight without getting up, eating food or taking medicine. She would sleep through any noise in the house, including someone dry bathing her. There really was nothing we could do to wake her.

I was very diligent about making sure that she did not get any bedsores in her back or sides. However, we failed to check her heels during one of her long sleeping episodes, this resulted in a bedsore that was hard for me to look at. To promote healing, our challenge was to keep her foot in a position such that her heels would not touch the bed. The hospice nurse brought a cushioned half bootie to help with positioning, but mom hated that. We ended up having to adjust pillows to keep her feet propped up while she was awake and we would put on those booties when she would fall asleep.

During those episodes, she had to be turned from side to side several times a day to prevent bedsores. Once she went into a coma for last ten days of her life, we had a schedule for turning her side to side every hour to prevent bedsores. We really needed round-the-clock caregivers to keep turning her and checking her adult diapers on almost hourly basis. I put myself in rotation to cover the shifts. It was both physically and emotionally challenging to see my mom so helpless.

Withholding Food and Water

Ruby

I thought it was counter intuitive and cruel to withhold water and food when the hospice nurse advised me to do that. Then my mom's hospice physician educated me how forcing food and water were just prolonging her pain and misery.

My mom had diabetes and we kept desserts away from her. But when she went on hospice, I started making or buying anything she felt like eating. One day I came home and mom was experiencing one of her dementia episodes.

"Did you bring Krispy Kreme glazed donuts for me?" She asked me.

"I didn't know that you wanted them," I responded.

"But I called you several times today to remind you."

I quizzically glanced at my mom's caregiver who shook her head indicating there had been no such calls. Understanding the situation, I told mom, "Oh I am so sorry, I wanted to take you for a drive and buy you fresh warm donuts, do you want to go?" And off we went to get her donuts.

As my mom got closer to death, she got less and less interested in eating and drinking. Most days, she did not even want her well-balanced diet shakes. So, I called her hospice physician to discuss what I should do. He told me to respect her wishes and to not force feed her.

"The lack of food and water will slow down her brain function, relax her and let her move on in peace," he told me. Accepting that providing nourishment at this stage of her life was counterproductive and was prolonging her misery was so contrary to what we had done with my mom for years. A few days after she stopped eating and drinking she went into a coma.

Safe Beauty Treatment

Mariya

Lisa found that not all salons were equipped well enough to handle someone in an extremely frail condition close to the end of their life.

Lisa visited her Aunty Mariya for her eighty-fifth birthday. The whole family knew by then that Aunt Mariya had at the most two more months to live. Her mom declared that they should give her a makeover.

"I have been thinking long and hard, how we can make the day special for Aunt Mariya. I think we should take her to a salon, get her a perm like she used to have when she was in her thirties. We should also get her a new outfit that is deep blue, since that is her favorite color. Then you can take some good portrait pictures of her. I think she would love that."

This plan sounded fun and doable for Lisa to accomplish during her two-day visit.

Lisa asked her mom, “Do you know what salon around here still does perms and can work with someone in Aunt Mariya’s condition?”

“Don’t all salons do that?” Lisa’s mom answered.

Lisa started calling the salons in the area to see where she could take her aunt. She found that very few salons did perms, and for the ones that did, they did not have an opening for the time Aunt Mariya was likely to be awake. Finally, she found one that had an opening but they were very reluctant about their ability to work with someone in Aunt Mariya’s mental and physical condition.

“To be very honest, I think you are better off taking your aunt to the salon in the Brookdale senior living community, it’s called PS LifeStyle. They are better equipped with facilities and staff for someone in your aunt’s condition.” the salon owner said.

“I would have never thought to look there, but it makes perfect sense,” Lisa responded.

When Lisa called the PS Lifestyle salon and shared with the manager, “This will be my Aunt’s last visit to a salon,” the manager responded that she would make this happen. After a quick hold, she came back on the phone and said, “We can do this, we will keep the salon open for you past our closing time. Do you want to also book an appointment for your mom for a haircut? We can also do a manicure and pedicure for all three of you, if you like."

We got Aunt Mariya in the car and went for a spa day immediately after the call. The stylist stations were so well-equipped to handle my Aunt's wheelchair, and the staff was so much at ease with talking to both Aunt Mariya and mom. As we were leaving the staff gave us all warm hugs. It was amazing to see such joy on two sisters faces as they looked at each other with deep affection and admiration saying, "You look so beautiful, you remind me of mom."

Lisa's mom told Lisa at Aunt Mariya's funeral, "Honey, the spa day picture you took is what I am keeping in my mind to get through this ceremony."

Monitoring a Loner

Noah

Lisa's loner dad would have considered someone watching him day and night a complete invasion of his privacy, but at the end of his life he didn't even notice.

Lisa's dad could not be left alone for the last six months of his life. Not only was he physically weak, but his judgment and memory were seriously impaired. He only recognized Lisa and her kids. His heart was very weak. He was on in-home hospice. A few times, Lisa thought about moving him into a facility. However, she did not have the heart to do so knowing that it was short-term and that the highlight of his day was the moment when his grandkids greeted him every morning or when they came home after school or other activities. His grandkids also adored the way he greeted them each time by singing, "Hello my dear, so glad to see you."

Lisa tried sensors that sounded an alarm when he moved out of bed but this did not work very well. The only option was to have someone watching him all day and night. She knew that he would have hated having someone around him all day along, let alone having a stranger sleeping in his bedroom at night. However, at this stage, he did not even notice.

Summary

This phase of our journey was when we could see the end was near, we could see the end in sight. There were moments of acceptance for what was going to be inevitable, and in these moments, we could sense the deep love we had for our seenagers bubble up. However, most of the time we were still going through the motions and getting the some of the most difficult tasks checked on our to-do lists.

Chapter 9 – Supporting End of Life

Freedom from a Failing Body

Don’t Leave Me

You are free of this failing body
I have to believe you no longer suffer
I wish I could make sure you are happy
Your worldly riches are still here
You left everything behind, even me
I keep sending my love to you
I hope you can feel how much I miss you
No longer do I have daily chores and worries for you
All I can do for you now is pray
I am a better person because of you
You taught me to be strong
You helped me face my fears
Wiped my tears
What if I need you if I fall
How will you celebrate my wins
How will I show you my love
Don’t go alone into the night
Don’t leave me

Getting Closure

Alli

My aunt's life ended with one thing that she had wanted for decades, an ultimate closure.

My aunt had lived a very difficult life, I would not wish the experiences she had on even my worst enemy. She truly had an epic closure for the end of her life. She had unresolved issues with her ex-husband. He had moved to Pakistan without telling her.

When it looked like her death was eminent, my dad shared with me with tears in his eyes, "I wish I had been able to find her ex-husband and bring him to see her now. She had told me a long time ago that for her peace she needed to see him one last time and understand why he treated her the way he did."

I called a friend of mine that was a private investigator and shared with him my aunt's wishes, I told him I would pay him handsomely if he were able to find that man. In just two days he was able to locate him and it turned out that he was living in the same city. I asked my friend to communicate my aunt's condition and her wishes to him. To my dad's and my surprise, he decided to come immediately after he heard from my friend.

When he entered her room, all of us had just stepped away for lunch. My dad recognized him getting in his car, as we were pulling into the hospital entrance after lunch. We found out from the nurse that he had stayed with my aunt for an hour. My aunt was sleeping when we entered her room, for the first time I saw a peaceful smile on her face.

My aunt received closure the moment she had that fateful conversation with her ex-husband.

About two hours later she was pronounced dead.

Last Acknowledgements

Sami

Even a little squeeze of my hand meant so much.

My uncle sat down with his attorney on the same day he handed me the "keys to his kingdom." He wanted to review everything in detail to make sure he had not changed his mind about anyone. He also made sure that his attorney, executor and friend (all rolled into one) had contact information for everyone in his will.

The day his physician told him that there was nothing else left to try and that he had a few more weeks to live, Uncle Sami declared "It's time for my death with dignity." His physician pulled out a form that we had to sign and then he wrote the prescription.

As I stood by his bedside talking to him, I broke down and apologized for the times I might have hurt him. I felt in my heart that with his slight squeeze of my hand he was acknowledging that he could hear me and was comforting me. His final squeeze brought more comfort to me than any praise he could showered on me.

Surrounded by All

Eli

My dad's wish was to leave a video message of gratitude for all his friends and family, and be surrounded by the closest ones. His wish came true.

The day I saw my dad not being able to breathe in the ER, I felt overwhelmed with the feeling of helplessness. It was like watching him drown in the ocean gasping for breath, while standing on the pier without any resources to get him out of the water.

As far as finding closure for my dad, I think that his last day on earth probably happened exactly the way he would have wanted. He had been on hospice for just three days. It was on a Wednesday afternoon when his daughters, sons-in-laws and grandkids all said goodbye in their own ways. He looked up at the ceiling and told mom that no one would understand what he was seeing.

"My body feels like it is sliding," my father said to the doctor as he walked in to check on dad.

"How close is he to leaving us?" I anxiously asked as I followed the doctor out of his room.

He explained with compassion, "He is probably hours away from leaving us. This is a common experience at this time. People also look towards the ceiling. He is doing that too."

Dad asked if we could turn his bed 180 degrees around to face the window. We moved everyone out of the room, and the nurse and I did just that. He closed his eyes, and he looked peaceful as if he was taking an afternoon nap.

An hour later, Uncle Tom, my dad's childhood best friend arrived from Nebraska.

"I think you just missed him, he closed his eyes less than an hour ago," I told Uncle Tom sadly. He sat down on a chair next to my dad. His pain and grief were palpable.

"I should have come earlier," he repeated over and over again. All of a sudden, my dad opened his eyes, looked at Uncle Tom, gave him a big smile and said, "I am so glad you came."

They started a joyful conversation that was filled with memories, laughter and love.

"Remember the times we used to sneak around and eat junk food?" Uncle Tom asked. "What was our nickname for junk food?" he asked my father. The two of them had the most amazing conversation.

My dad responded, grinning ear to ear, "It was Hum All Hum Man Hum." He added with the facial expression of a man sitting on a front porch sipping a cold beer and reminiscing about old times.

My dad started telling the story of how they had come up with the nickname, "Do you recall the day? We had six bottles of coke, a handful of Kit-Kat and a big bag of potato chips. Your mom came looking for us and we tried to hold the loot in bags behind us. When she asked what we were holding behind our back, we babbled hum all hum man hum. We were trying to figure out whether to lie, run or confess. "Hold your hands up front!" she demanded. We dropped what was in our hands and ran."

Looking directly at me with smiles he added "From that moment on, we always referred to junk food as *Hum All Hum Man Hum.*"

Uncle Tom and my father both laughed out loud and talked energetically.

If someone had overheard their conversation, they would have never believed that one of them was experiencing failing heart and lungs and would be dead within minutes of that conversation. After 20 minutes, my dad said he was very tired and closed his eyes.

The nurse turned off the monitor in his room and told us she was monitoring him from her desk, and would let us know when he passed. Not knowing how fast his condition was deteriorating, I went to the restroom and took my time to come back to the room, just to get a little break. When I came back, the nurse was already by his bedside, she looked at me and pronounced matter-of-factly, "he is dead." I really wanted to scream and say, "I really wanted to by my dad's bedside when he passed. That is why I have not left the hospital for last two days." Instead I just broke down. To this day, I am mad that I let her turn the monitor off in my father's room.

Given the extreme generosity of my parents, I had always assumed they would be organ donors. But to my surprise, they both were horrified at the idea when I brought up the subject some time ago.

I was terrified at the idea of having to bury my dad. In the last ten years of his life, he had begun experiencing claustrophobia. His pulmonologist had shared an interesting theory with me expressing that the COPD resulting in his difficulty breathing, could in fact be a catalyst for his claustrophobia.

I had to take meds to get through his burial. When he was being lowered into the grave, I wanted to scream, "Stop! My dad is claustrophobic! Please don't bury him!" But I refrained. I had been confiding my feelings about burying him with a friend. She eased my anxiety as they lowered his casket into the ground by whispering in my ears, "Your dad's soul was caged inside his physical body.

Remember that he is free and released into the vastness of beauty, love and peace. They are only burying his physical body which was the cause of his suffering." I found comfort in those words.

In my wildest dreams, I would not have expected him to die before my mom, as he was such a dedicated and caring husband and really an exemplary caregiver. Yet he did. He died two years before mom.

Prolonged Ending

Ruby

I really do not know what is worse, not being able to say goodbye to someone before they pass or saying goodbye not knowing if that is truly the last time over and over again.

I felt that I was on a roller coaster during the last nine months of my mom's life in hospice care. I rarely knew what to expect from one day to the next. Three months into this time period, the hospice doctor told me that my mother would most likely die within a week. My brother flew in from Texas. My mom rallied, but then reached a new low a few weeks later.

I did not want to be accused of crying wolf, so for the next six months, I became very selective in sharing what was going on, even if it became very close. I did not want pity, lectures or judgment from other family members. I had no time or energy for any of that. In fact, I had very little time or energy even for my children, husband, home, career, health, and a handful of friends. I know that I dropped many balls on a daily basis. Sometimes I forgot something my husband asked me to do or I did not remember a meeting I had scheduled or I forgot to call the pharmacy for medication refill.

I rarely broke down and cried. Taking care of my emotional needs never made it to the top of my daily “to do” list. I was barely getting through the “must dos” for the day. With the reality of having so much on my plate, crying felt like a luxury I could not afford.

My mom lived in hospice for a total of nine months and kept declining every few weeks. Every new low made me think that this was the end of her life. But somehow, she would magically continue to push through. The hospice team supporting my mom and I kept wondering what was keeping her here. For every new low, I would think to myself, “It can’t get worse than this.” But yet, it would. I would stop by her room every time I was leaving home. In the back of my mind, I always had the nagging thought that this was maybe the last conversation I would ever have with her. It was too difficult to say that many goodbyes.

One of my friends said to me one day, “It was really painful that I was not able to say goodbye to my mom before she passed.”

“This will probably sound insane to you, but I am not sure what is more painful: not being able to say goodbye or wondering every day for months if that morning’s goodbye as I left the house or that evening's goodnight when I was going to sleep was finally my last one," I told my friend.

I had many conversations with the hospice team where I wondered what was keeping her here. I prayed for guidance on what closure she needed so she could move on. One by one, family and friends visited, trying to provide her with closure.

Some of them said things like, "We are sorry we were not able to do as much for you as we would have liked." Or "I still remember the day I did … That must have been hurtful. I hope you will forgive me."

I started to think about what was unresolved in our relationship. It turned out that I did not feel that I had done enough for my mom. I felt that I had not quite fulfilled the promise I had made to my dad on his deathbed when I had said, "I will take care of mom, it is okay for you to let go." I felt that I should have found better caregivers for her, spent more time with her, kept her more active and engaged. I think she stayed long enough to give me a chance to work through those feelings, and convince myself that I really did the best I could, given the situation.

My mom started talking about wanting to go home in the last couple of months of her life. One time she was so insistent that I got her in the wheelchair and told her we were going to walk to her home. At one point, she told me to take a turn and go right to get home. "We can't get home by going straight," she said, convinced that we were actually heading to her old house. The reality was that the home she so wanted to get to was half way around the world in Asia and we were walking in my neighborhood in San Diego. I started talking to her about her trip on an African safari. My mother was immediately transported back into the past and began describing the animals she saw and all of the details of her trip many years ago. As she was completely immersed in her memories, I wheeled her chair home. As soon as we entered the home, I started to see annoyance on her face and before she could realize what I was doing, I handed her the giraffe that she bought for me on that safari. Her stories continued as I returned her safely back in her bed and waited for her to fall asleep.

My mom said only three hurtful words to me in my whole life. The day my mother told me, "I hate you" was one of the toughest days of my life. But I had to remind myself that she did not even remember who I was. I had gone to her room to say goodbye as I was going out with my daughter to Girl Scouts meeting for a couple of hours. My only response to her as I hid my tears was, "It is okay mom, but you know I love you." The next day, things were normal and she did not remember saying those hurtful words to me.

There were too many episodes of dementia and the frequency and intensity of the episodes increased. I had read books and talked to specialists enough to know that it is best not to challenge someone experiencing dementia. I knew that the best approach was to go along with their story and build from it, to make them feel heard and keep them peaceful. "I must meet her in her world" was my internal mantra when she had one of those episodes.

I must say that the most difficult episodes were when she did not remember that my father had died. One day she said to me, "Your father just walked by my bedroom door, I yelled at him to come and help me and he ignored me." My mother was very upset and asked me to go and get him immediately. "He just left, Mom," I told her.

"Where did he go? How could he leave without saying goodbye?" She cried. For several hours, she continued asking why my father was still not back. The next day she clearly remembered that he had been dead for almost two years. I asked her about the night prior and she was surprised that she had not remembered he was dead. Similar episodes happened many other times, and I actually never had the heart to remind her during those times that her loving husband who treated her like Queen-Bee was in fact dead.

Due to Parkinson's disease, my mother had been experiencing nightmares for the past ten years; but about two months before she passed away, she started screaming out loud in pain and grief. Her facial expressions were gut wrenching as if someone was torturing her. This new pain went beyond the discomfort she experienced during her recurring nightmares. Now, her cries resembled blood-curling screams. When she woke up, my mother would not remember that she was dreaming and she often did not know that she had been in pain. Watching someone you love in that kind of agony, without being able to know why or what you can do about it, felt like a very harsh punishment.

By the end, we were really having a difficult time keeping her pain-free and comfortable. Finding the right dosage and giving it at the right time seemed to be an art. During that time, I got a viral infection and had 103 degree fever for a couple of weeks. One of the paid caregivers did not seem to understand the concept of "comfort care" and refused to give my mother morphine. One night, while my fever was 104 degrees and mom was screaming in pain so loudly that the neighbors could hear her, I went down and asked Joann if she could give my mother some morphine. I didn't want to touch her in case I was contagious. Joann not only refused to do so, but added, "You are doing mercy killing and I don't want to have any part of that." Needless-to-say we parted ways at the crack of dawn.

Right before her death, my mother was in a coma for ten days and every day we thought would be her last. Her feet started purple and black mottling. I was informed by hospice that this is a sign that death is very near. This process went on for three days.

A few days before the end, my daughter asked me, "Mom if grandma dies in this room, will you ever be able to enter it again?"

"Yes, honey," I told her. "I will, because I will always feel her presence in this room and that will be comforting to me."

I could tell from my daughter's expression that she did not understand the sentiment. I didn't feel like I had enough strength however to prolong this difficult exchange. Just then I recalled a conversation with my mom at a family friend's funeral when she told me that she really did not think it had been a good idea for the grandkids to have experienced their grandma's last dying breath. "The kids looked like they were traumatized. Don't you think?" she had said. "I would never want my grandkids to see me die." I could not help but wonder whether this was the reason why my mother was hanging on.

So, I called the nearest skilled nursing facility (called Brookdale) and asked them if they would take her. They assured me what I was asking for was not unusual. The hospice team arranged for five days of respite care to be paid for by the insurance company.

It had only taken six hours from the moment I had the thought until the ambulance came to take my mom to skilled nursing. I had asked for a room big enough for me to stay with her. The whole time I suppressed the nagging voice inside of me telling me *you're kicking your own mom out of your home as she is dying, you are abandoning her.* I ignored the voice and went to my closet and took out a big suitcase and packed it with everything I thought I would need to stay with mom for a few days. "I am not going to leave your side mom," I whispered as I packed.

When the ambulance scheduler from hospice called to arrange for her transfer late that afternoon, she said to me, "I am so sorry to say this, but I think it is important to tell you that your mom may not survive the ride to the nursing home. I know it's less than five miles from your home, but I have seen this before."

I was driving behind the ambulance, close enough to be able to see the paramedics sitting in the back with mom. Half way there I could see that they were getting into action. I wondered what was going on. When the ambulance parked at the Nursing home, I parked right behind them and ran to the ambulance. When I looked at one of the paramedics, he said, "She has no pulse." They took her to the room my mom and I were going to spend her last precious hours and days together. The doctor came right away and pronounced her dead.

My mom had always had a fear of being out of her home alone at night. This had stemmed from living in a city with crimes taking place at night. This fear was never an issue when she was younger but as she got older, her phobia grew exponentially. While I was growing up and even when I was an adult, my mother would often worry about me whenever I was out after dark.

My mother died after sun down. I had to sign papers to have the funeral home take her body around 11 pm. I remember numbing my emotions in order to get through that signature and to see her body be wheeled out and taken into a van.

We wanted to have the funeral and burial done quickly, but it was the day before New Year's Eve. It was so hard to make arrangements during the holiday. We had trouble getting almost everything arranged, from the funeral service to the burial, but finally we were able to get all the plans in place. The day arrived, and as I said goodbye to my mom and caressed her fragile hand one last time, I was overcome with emotions. I was numb going through the service and burial.

I have healed from countless traumatic experiences in my life. I know time does heal, and the feelings are not as intense but this pain is still very raw for me two years later.

The day after my mom was buried, my brother and I went through everything in my mom's room and gave most of it away to charity. Looking back, it was probably the best time to do this. Being in a state of shock made it easier to get through this process. This reminded me of my mom telling me about the time she had gone through my grandmother's belongings with her, five years before my grandmother passed away. The two of them had meticulously tagged each item with the name of a child, grandchild, friend or charity as recipient of the item after my grandmother's death.

Two weeks prior to her death, my mom removed the last piece of jewelry she was wearing, and insisted I put it on right there and then.

We took out a few things to give to the grandkids. We had done the same thing when my dad had passed. At that time, the youngest grandchild was too young to understand the emotional value of what he had received. I found it very endearing when he came to me after we had given him one thing to remember his grandmother by, and asked me, "If you can find me one more thing that belonged to Grandma that I could have, I would really like that." I gave him her prayer beads and he was extremely joyful. Later as we were going for a prayer service, my son took out a hat that had belonged to my dad. The same grandchild smelled his cap and declared, "This smells like Grandpa, I really like it." My son gave him the hat.

Doula for End of Life

Mariya

Lisa's cousins gave a very elaborate and professionally planned send off to their mom.

Lisa's cousin and his wife were very much into making sure that the community, family and friends all thought highly of them. They also could not be bothered about planning details of Aunt Mariya's funeral. So, they hired an end of life planning doula. Lisa said that the funeral and service were both exceptionally well planned and highly respectful of her aunt. Lisa said to her mom sitting in the service, "At least they were willing to spend the money, no matter what their motives were. I was worried that it would end up being just the two of us for the funeral. I am so glad for Aunt Mariya that they stepped up. The doula really knew what she was doing, making sure Aunt Mariya's wishes were taken into account for the service and funeral."

"Aunt Mariya got a good funeral and that is all that matters. Plus, her son and daughter-in-law are making a great show of how much they cared for her to impress their friends and neighbors."

"Never judge honey," said her mom lovingly, "judgement of others is a confession of our own character."

Ending Life on His Terms

Noah

Lisa's dad wanted things his way when he was alive and controlled the way his life ended.

Before his death, Lisa asked his dad's hospice chaplain to mediate a conversation between his mom and dad. They both needed that for closure. Her mom felt that for the first time he acknowledged how much she had really meant to him when he said, "I have loved you from the first day I met you, you brought things into my life that I would have never been able to myself, you made my life richer and I will always be grateful for that." This conversation happened two months before he passed, and Lisa could tell that he was different after that, almost as if a big burden had been lifted of his shoulders.

Lisa saw the most pain in her mom and dad's eyes and heard it in their voices when she had to help them relieve and clean them up. Her parents expressed gratitude, humility but also sadness that they had to put their daughter in a position to help them in such a vulnerable way. Lisa could not help but think and contrast the many times when she was a baby and how her parents had gladly done the same for her so many years ago.

Lisa's dad suffered with tremendous pain because of his spine all the time. There was not enough medication the doctor could prescribe as far as he was concerned. Lisa could not tell if his pain made his depression worse or if his depression made his pain worse, but they were certainly feeding on each other. On days when the pain was bad he would refuse to eat anything. He would sit in front of the TV in his room and flip channels constantly as he would find nothing interesting or amusing. It was hard to watch her father that way. When Lisa was a kid, she was a picky eater with very little appetite. Her dad would always find something that would entice Lisa into eating. Lisa on the other hand could not entice her dad to eat anything. She could not even force him to drink Ensure for nutrition.

Lisa recalled her father frequently being judgmental about her mom's dad, who had suffered from terrible depression after he retired. He was a classic example of someone who felt he did not have any purpose in life now that he was no longer working. Her dad would often say about her grandfather, "If he wasn't this lazy or proud, he would get off the sofa and get a part-time job or volunteer, he could improve his health and not be a burden to the entire family." It was ironic that Lisa's dad would have probably said the same things about himself if he had been able to be objective about the last few years of his own life.

Lisa says this is one of the hardest lessons that her dad's life has taught her. "Sometimes, it seems that our worst fears about life can come to fruition in those last moments of our lives. This was certainly the case for my dad who had judged others for being a burden on their family members, only to find himself in the same situation at the end of his life."

Lisa's dad was on hospice, and his ordeal went on for about two years. During that time, he progressively became quieter and more subdued. In the last two weeks of his life, it was almost as if he had a new lease on life. He seemed more content. Lisa was paying someone to take him out of the house in a wheelchair every day for half an hour. Many days, the paid caregiver would come to take him out of the house and her dad would either refuse or act like he was asleep. However, the last day of his life he asked Lisa several times whether the caregiver was coming to take him for a walk or not. He told Lisa, "Today I would like to go on the walking path that goes through the forest. Can the caregiver take me for a two-hour walk? I feel like fresh air." Lisa was so pleasantly surprised and shocked by his behavior that she did not question his motives.

When two hours had passed and they were still not back from the walk, Lisa called the caregiver. She told Lisa that her father had her stop at the entrance of the walking path and told her he wanted to take a nap. She said, "He is sleeping so quietly, with such a peaceful look on his face that I don't feel like moving his wheelchair or talking around him."

"I hate the way I am destroying my loving daughter's life," he would often say to Lisa. On that day he took matters in his own hands and overdosed on his pain medicine. This was his way of obtaining his own closure. He did not want to die in Lisa's home because he thought that "death in a house brings down its value." So, he made sure he was out of her house when he passed.

Piece of Her for Everyone

Aliya

Lisa's mom life was about sharing and giving, she made sure that at the end of her life she was leaving something for everyone to remember her by.

Lisa's mom and dad had disposed of most of their belongings when they sold their home, all except her mom's collections. Her mom loved shopping for costume jewelry and she had boxes full of them. Lisa's mom had her move all of that in a storage facility along with some of her antique furniture. Some of that was good and most of it was not. It took Lisa weeks to sort through all of that make a list and work with her mom to figure out what she wanted to do with it. In her mom's eyes, it was all valuable and Lisa should not just give it away to charity. She wanted to make sure that everyone she knew got something from her collection to "remember me by."

After Lisa's aunt and dad passed away, Lisa's mom moved in with her. One day when her mom walked back from an event at church, she was gasping for breath. Lisa took one look at her mom and stopped her in her tracks.

She called an ambulance and her mom was taken to the hospital immediately. As it turned out, her mom was experiencing a heart attack. She stayed in the hospital for a few weeks, going in and out of surgery because of complications. Lisa used to call her "my mom, the Energizer Bunny, because like the commercial she keeps going and going and going…," since that commercial always reminded her of her mom who "keeps going and going…"

One day while Lisa was sitting by her mom's bedside in the hospital room, with her mom in very critical condition, the same Energizer Bunny commercial started to play on TV. As the commercial came to an end, her mom's heart rate monitor also flatlined.

Lisa thought to herself, "She was the Energizer Bunny who was going to take care of everyone around her, so many people depended on her, how could she leave without making sure her loved ones weren't going to be lonely without her?"

I guess that is the reason why Lisa reached out to all of her mom's relatives and friends when her mom passed, even the ones that Lisa herself did not appreciate. It was not just to reduce their loneliness but also her own.

Lisa's mom had a positive attitude about life. Over the years there was nothing anyone could say to bring her down, and in fact

Lisa always saw her mom smiling. However, when her mom spent the last two weeks of her life in the hospital, she seemed very depressed. Lisa really wanted her mom to finish her life on a good note. Lisa worked very hard to have the people that her mom had issues with to come and visit her, including her cousin and his wife. Unfortunately, her mom was clinically depressed at the end and Lisa still regrets to this day that she could not do anything to change the bleak view of her mom's world. It is hard for Lisa to digest the fact that her mom, who lived a happy and giving life, actually left the world sad and feeling lonely at the end. Several experts have consoled her by saying, "Your mom was not who you saw in the last few weeks of her life. Remember her for who she truly was, a giving, loving and joyful soul." They would sometimes add, "There is nothing more you could have done for her. She is free from the body that failed her at the end."

Summary

When caring for a loved one, it is nearly impossible to live free of the guilt of falling short as a caregiver. One day when I was filling out a customer satisfaction survey, it occurred to me that I should have my seenagers give me feedback on how I was performing as a caregiver in their eyes.

I had poignant conversations about the quality of my caregiving with both my mom and dad. At some point when the end was near, I talked to them about if they were happy with their present surroundings and if there was anything else I could do to make them more comfortable. I shared with them the areas of guilt I was carrying and things I wished I had done differently for them. Both of them assured me that they truly believed that I had done much more for them than they expected. My mom told me that I had done lot more for her than she ever did for her mother.

I wish I had similar conversations with my aunt and uncle.

On most days, Lisa feels that she did the best she could, given the circumstances that she was dealt. She has additional regrets centered around not getting enough information about her seenagers and their family histories to pass on to the next generations.

Chapter 10 – Grieving After Death

The Flood of Emotions, the Tears of Grief, the End of the Journey

My hat is off to you for choosing to take on the caregiver role or even if you are just planning for it. It is a role that you will treasure; likely not while you are in it, but definitely in hindsight.

Guilt

The times we were not there to meet their needs and the times we got angry at them now keep us up at night.

With our conversations Lisa and I have been able to help each other see that we did the best job as caregivers given the time, energy, resources and skills we had. There were times we could not be there for them physically or emotionally because our platter was too full. We do believe that our loved ones would forgive us for that.

However, we both have stories about angry emotional outbursts at each of our seenagers. Sometimes we just could not tolerate what they were doing, sometimes we were just frustrated.

Every time I am driving on Interstate 5 and pass exit 51B, a flood of tears gush out of my eyes.

This is where I had yelled at my dad for telling me "Just forgive your cousin…" I had not even let him finish the sentence. Now it doesn't even matter what my cousin had done. What matters is the way I had responded with the outburst, "Don't you dare tell me…"

My voice was harsh, and I went on for a couple of minutes till the exit light went green and I was on the freeway. I know this is the worst way I had ever talked to my dad. I recall my mom telling me in her gentle voice, "Honey, I don't think you should talk to your dad like that." I had stayed quiet the rest of the drive. I don't think I ever apologized for that.

The very next day, my dad had a heart attack and then the chain reaction of his health decline started. I don't know if my emotional vomit triggered his heart attack, or it was a coincidence. I guess it does not matter at this time.

I just wish I could get an opportunity to re-live that interaction and handle it differently.

Loss

The firsts were very hard: the holidays, the birthdays, the anniversaries. It is all hard.

My mom died on a Saturday night and the first time I really broke down was the following Saturday night.

Not having my parents with me for my birthday, the first year after they died was probably the toughest of the "firsts" for me.

Even when I totally expected it.

Even though they were driving me crazy while they were alive.

Even though it is good to know they are pain free.

Even though I have a lot more free time, and a lot fewer responsibilities.

Even though my spouse and kids are happier that they have more of my attention.

Even though I can get back to focusing on my life.

I still cry and breakdown from time to time.

The frequency of breaking down has gradually decreased, and the heaviness of the heart has somewhat lessened.

Someone recently reminded me that it was okay to cry, and okay to grieve because when a parent dies you lose a "lifeline." I think what they meant was that you lose your lineage to the past, your connections to your ancestors.

However, maybe they meant something more. A few months ago, I was visiting a friend who had just come out of a minor surgery. I know that friend's mom is a worrywart. As I was about to leave her hospital room, I asked her, "Does your mom know about your surgery?"

"Oh yes, both mom and dad! They flew in yesterday morning, they were in the hospital ever since I checked in yesterday for the surgery, I had to throw a little temper tantrum to send them home," she responded. No sooner had she completed her sentence, I felt my eyes welling up, and the demons in my head started reminding me, "If you are in that situation, you will no longer have a lifeline."

Flood of Memories

Lisa and I are often both flooded with memories that get triggered by the smallest of reminders.

Seeing their favorite flower, sitting where they sat before, eating their favorite meal or celebrating holidays. Four weeks after my mom passed I got really dressed and went to a concert. I wanted to feel like I was going somewhere fun to celebrate.

I had gone with family members visiting from out of town. I twisted my ankle as soon as I got out of the car. I found it devastating that no one really cared to slow down and walk with me or was compassionate enough to ask if I needed any help. Even though I was limping I found the rest of the family walking well ahead of me all engrossed in conversation about a trip to Europe they were planning on taking. I felt a twinge of hurt, and recalled that if my parents were here with me, they would have made an overwhelming fuss over it and would have wanted to drive me right to the entrance of the concert hall. My mom would have asked me to lean on her as I walked. I realized then that I was no longer anyone's dear daughter.

The concert had singers and dancers from all over the world. There was a thirteen-year-old dancer who was introduced by her mom, who was also a very accomplished dancer herself. As she introduced her daughter, one could sense the pride she felt for her daughter. She said, “I don’t know how my daughter does this dance, I was not half as good at her age.” Even though I looked visibly calm and composed, every ounce of my being burst into tears. I would never have anyone in the world be as proud of me ever again as my parents always had been.

Dreams

I have had a lot of intense dreams of visitation, nightmares and just reliving the trauma of my seenagers lives. Most times I wake up in the morning exhausted because of them.

The majority of my dreams are replaying the experiences I had as a caregiver. However, with one big difference this time: I could sense and feel the pain of watching my loved one's suffering. Whereas, when they were alive, I had to go through the motions of the tasks at hand. There was no time or energy at that time to deal with my emotions. However, reliving those experiences in my dreams was much harder as I dealt with my own emotions and feelings.

One day I had a dream where I was walking on very colorful eggshells. The only way to get to my destination was to walk over them. I kept cracking eggshells as I went forward in spite of my strong will to do no harm. I kept trying to levitate with no success. My heart was full of anxiety and my body was shaking in fear of messing up and breaking another eggshell. This dream, like other dreams in general, had crazy transitions. I went from the walking on eggshells to dreaming about my mom falling and breaking her neck. I then transitioned back to the eggshell walk. Then I transitioned to watching my father unable to breathe in the ER and back to walking on eggshells.

Night after night, my nightmares continued. I would run away frantically from dinosaurs or tigers. I'd fight for my life as I was picked up in a tornado or would find myself driving in my car as the brakes gave out! Every morning as soon as my eyes would open, I would pick up the iPad carefully placed on my bedside table without moving too much. I have found that sometimes movement after waking up makes me forget the dream, while leaving me feeling overwhelmed and drained. I would not go to same website every time to find the interpretation of the dream. Rather, I would do a general Google search with key words describing what I saw in the dream, whatever websites would show up on the top of the search list, would probably give me the closest interpretation of my dream. I have always believed that dreams and coincidences happen for a reason.

Even though each dream had a slightly different interpretation, the common thread throughout all of them was emotional turmoil.

Finally, one day I could have sworn that I heard a little animal running through bushes in our large two-acre backyard while being chased by a roaring bigger animal. Then I heard a moan and a deep bone-chilling cry. I woke up with that sound still reverberating in my head. I said to my husband who had not quite fallen asleep yet, "Did you hear that?" He responded, sounding puzzled, "Hear what?"

Given that this was a dream that seemed more real than any others and it really devastated me, I spent that day thinking hard about what it and all the previous dreams were trying to tell me. I came to the conclusion that evening that the dream was trying to tell me that my emotional turmoil and fears were killing who I am. This convinced me that I needed some counseling to help me with my emotional and spiritual crisis. The very next day I met Lisa.

Seeking Help

Seeking help is not a sign of weakness, whether the help is from a professional, family or friend. You just need to learn how to ask.

Unlike me, Lisa was very unapologetic about facing and expressing her feelings. She wasn't shy about asking for help from her immediate family. She felt no shame in going for counseling and taking antidepressants.

Lisa also wanted to change all of her surroundings and start a new life with a clean slate. She went on a mission to find a new exciting job in a new city. Since her husband travelled a lot and could live in any city (as long as he lived closed to an airport) they had no strong ties to any specific region.

Lisa had taken full charge of her parents' needs and had also become extremely vested in her aunt's well-being. With those goals as her focus, she had no tolerance for others in the family who were sitting on the sidelines pontificating on what was the right course of care for her parents might be and only calling her when it suited them to give her advice. From her view if they could not be there through the roughest phase of her life, let alone her parent's lives, she had no time or energy for them. She had seen her parents do so much for both sides of the family all of her life. One small example of that was her mom putting her own life on hold to help her aunt. She was very disappointed to see that when crisis hit her parents, no one was there with compassion and support.

What amazed me about Lisa was that even though her extended family had disappointed her so many times in her journey as a caregiver, she decided that she would ask for little things that they could do for her in her period of grieving. She asked her family to return her calls within twenty-four hours if she left a message. She asked them to make sure they remembered to wish her a happy birthday. She asked them to donate money to her mom's favorite charity in lieu of flowers.

She said that she regrets that she did not accept her extended family for who they are, and what they would be willing or able to do while her parents were alive. "It would have saved me from carrying that anger for which I had no time or energy. At the same time, I could have probably got some help, rather than no help."

The Void

The time we were spending to take care of our seenagers is now available to be filled. Making a wise choice about how we fill the void will go a long way to recovery.

Lisa filled the void in her life with lots of new beginnings, a new city, new home, new job, new hobbies and above all new friends.

I, on the other hand, am filling the void by writing this book. I am also trying to volunteer with a number of non-profits working on improving the quality of life of seenagers.

We both know that we cannot bring our loved ones back. We both know that we have to move on and make our lives richer in other ways.

We have also realized the toll that the journey took on our own personal health. Now we are learning to be the champions and advocates for our health.

Summary

If I had to sum up in one word the lesson I've learned as a caregiver it would be: COMPASSION.

What would I do differently for myself to make it easier to cope with the challenges as a caregiver? COMPASSION.

What do I miss the most about my seenagers? COMPASSION.

Valuable References

Please visit www.villagecore.org for valuable resources for caregivers.

About the Author

On February 15, 1985 when I left Pakistan to come to the United States of America, there were thirty-four people from my "village" that came to the airport. They wanted to spend my last moments in Pakistan with me. I was the first one in our close-knit village to move oceans away. I knew then that this moment was going to be a treasured memory for the rest of my life.

But it didn't strike me how special it was until twenty-five years later when I went back to Pakistan. This time only my parents came to the airport. In the most populous city in Pakistan my parents became isolated because many of their family and friends had passed away and others had immigrated. It hit me hard that my parents did not have a village to take care of them. I knew then that I would have to become their primary caregiver as they aged.

Amazingly, history was repeating itself. My grandparents had a wonderful village, and in fact everyone who knew my dad was tired of hearing his stories about how wonderful it was to live in that small town in India. Just like my parents, my grandparents had lost their village as they grew older. In 1947 India split into two countries: India for Hindus and Pakistan for Muslims. Large numbers of Muslims moved from India to Pakistan. My dad and his brothers were among the many who immigrated. My grandparents immigrated to Pakistan when they were finally unable to take care of themselves in India.

After the move, my dad tried with his parents (as I tried with mine) to recreate the village that they had lost - but neither of us was very successful.

So, in 2007 when I owned hair salons, two ladies approached me for my business expertise. They wanted to create a "Village" in Tierrasanta, based on the success of Beacon Hill Village that was highlighted in the AARP Bulletin "Long-Term Care Declaration of Independents - Home is where you want to live forever. Here's how. By Barbara Basler, December 2005." This new aging-in-place solution, set up as a grass roots non-profit, would connect members in a community to help each other. It would turn the community into a Village.

I loved the concept and having lived in a Village and lost it, recreating a "Village" sounded like a wonderful thing to be involved in. We formed the Village in 2008 with a powerhouse of energetic people, and I stayed on board as their president until the end of 2013. We grew Tierrasanta Village to almost 200 members. These members were there for each other for both support and play. Any Village gatherings I attended were always heartwarming and reminded me of my family and their supportive villages.

I have done a lot of different things in my career. With a degree in electrical engineering, I have worked in the information technology field for over twenty-five years, for Fortune 100 and midsize companies. I have owned hair salons and started other entrepreneurial ventures. However, I must say that one of the biggest highlights and challenges of my life has been taking care of my loved ones as they aged. I have learned a lot from my parents, aunt, and friends.

I have also learned a lot over the last ten years by volunteering in various roles for the Village Movement, San Diego Senior Alliance, Aging 2.0 etc. I have also tried to start both for profit and non-profit ventures in this tough space.

Through all my involvement with Aging related non-profits, I have found it amazing that even older adults have an easier time funding or donating to children's causes, than supporting initiatives that would help seniors. Perhaps the reason is that we want to stay in denial that we are all aging.

I am certainly determined to embrace my old age, white hair and all...

Yasmin Zahra Shah

52183269R00155

Made in the USA
San Bernardino, CA
13 August 2017